TRUST CUES

7 Hidden Factors That Inspire

Connection, **Credibility**,

and **Confidence**

PAT QUINN

Story **BUILDERS** P R E S S

Table of Contents

CHAPTER 1

All Relationships Are Built on Trust

I'm sitting in an auditorium with 1,000 people, all of us excited to see a group of speakers at a large national conference. Every person in the audience has come here today to hear these speakers, to learn from them, and perhaps make a purchase.

This isn't just any leadership conference; this is the kind of conference around which you plan your summer. Everyone is keyed-up to go because the organizers feature the best of the best global speakers all in one place. Tickets sell out fast, and this year is no different. I was fortunate to not only get a ticket but also a good seat near the front.

The lights in the auditorium dim as the first speaker takes the stage. Typical entry: The speaker is smiling, waving at the audience, and glancing back at the title screen of his presentation, waiting for the chatter to die down. And then he starts speaking. As I listen, though, I realize that something is off. I don't entirely believe everything he is saying. I see the evidence on the screen behind him, and I hear—or think I hear—a certain amount of conviction in his voice, but there is a palpable disconnect between the person on the stage and me there in my seat—and I'm not alone.

I look to my left and to my right and see that the people around me are also showing signs of disconnect. Some have started shuffling around and fidgeting. Others are looking anywhere but at the stage. It's not that his presentation is bad. The speaker is doing things according to typical public speaking practices, but none of us are with him. For some reason, it's just not working.

Forty-five minutes later, another speaker takes the stage. The energy in the room resets, and we're ready to try again. This time, we're rewarded. From the moment the presenter walks onto the stage, there is a shared feeling of connection between him and us. When I look around me this time, I see people leaning in, taking notes, listening intently, and believing every word that comes out of the speaker's mouth.

What is the difference between these two speakers? It's simple: *trust.*

The first speaker never gained the trust of the audience, and while his presentation had all the usual keynote elements, the message didn't resonate with us, and we weren't emotionally invested—at all. The second speaker also incorporated all the right elements, but there was something else going on, a cue we picked up as the audience, which created that trust factor between us.

As a speaking coach for the past couple of decades, I'm always interested in how people present themselves and their ideas and what works or doesn't work. I've watched countless presentations and worked with thousands of individuals from unknown sales people to celebrities and beyond, teaching them how to connect with their audience—*how to build trust.* In that time, I've seen some phenomenal communicators, people who capture the audience from the first sentence, and I've seen presenters who lose the audience right away.

This dynamic plays out on stages everywhere as speakers address audiences, but it also occurs one on one. Salespeople want the prospect sitting across the table from them to trust them. Service providers want their clients to trust them. Medical professionals want their patients, leaders, and teams to trust them. Teachers want their students' trust. It's all about trust. Every person who has run a business, every person who has tried to help another person, and every person who tries to serve diligently wants trust from the people they are talking to.

That's what this book is about—building trust in communication no matter the situation. Without trust, you've lost your audience before you've even started.

Trust Is Not a Fixed Element

There are great people in the world who have life-changing messages, but many of them are actually sabotaging their efforts without even realizing it by how they're presenting themselves and their message. But when they can't seem to get the results they want, they become convinced that there is nothing they can do to become better at helping people to really "get" what they're trying to say. But nothing could be further from the truth if they would just learn how to build trust.

Trust is about reliability, integrity, and truthfulness. It's a feeling built between two people who believe the other person has their best interest at heart. It's one of the most important elements in a relationship, no matter the type of relationship. If you don't trust the person across from you, there's no way forward with that person, and so you walk away.

While there is an element of subjectivity in trust, there are simple steps any person can take to increase the level of trust they inspire in their listener. Whether you spend most of your time speaking one on one to other people or speaking to groups of people, understanding the factors that create trust can make a huge difference in your effectiveness. Not only will you be more effective, but you will also help the people you are speaking with to be more successful.

Even Experts Have Things to Learn

Before I coached speakers, I was a high school math teacher. I'd always been good at math. It came easily to me. So technically, I should've been a really good math teacher. While I could show students how to do the work and teach them the concepts and formulas, give quizzes and tests, and lecture about calculus until I was blue in the face, I wasn't getting results as good as the other math teachers were. For a couple years, I couldn't figure out why. If I was technically smarter in the subject matter, why were my students' scores lower than Ms. Smith's class down the hall?

It came down to the same reason the first speaker at the conference lost us before reaching the main point of the presentation. I wasn't building trust with my "audience."

Once I started observing how the other teachers did what they did, I noticed that they spent time building trust with their students. They knew about the students' lives and school activities. They engaged with them in a way I hadn't.

Here's why it worked. The thing about learning is that when you learn something new, you are trying something you may or may not be successful at. In order to do that, alone or in front of others like a class of your peers, you have to trust that the teacher will help you and not humiliate you, that your peers won't hold this over your head all year, and that it's okay to be unsuccessful.

It wasn't that I had intentionally been creating mistrust with my students; it's that I hadn't been aware of all the ways I failed to capitalize on *building* trust.

After figuring out how other teachers built trust in their classrooms, I shifted my focus from teaching technically perfectly to teaching very well while leaving room for building trust. And it made all the difference.

The Seven Factors of Building Trust

When you know how to build trust quickly, it changes everything. It makes you more effective as a speaker and a professional. It affects every relationship you are in. Parents are better parents when their kids trust them. Bosses are better bosses when their employees trust them. Sales professionals are more effective when the people they are speaking to trust them.

Whether you are in a sales conversation, a coaching conversation, a private conversation, or a personal discussion, there are specific things you can do to increase trust between you and the other person. Conversely, there are things you can do to decrease trust. My goal in writing this book is to ensure that you are aware of the specific actions you can take to foster trust, no matter the scenario.

Throughout my professional career, I have found seven factors that cause people to trust you. Certainly, you could work on any of these seven factors in isolation, but when you combine them, it amplifies the power of every conversation and helps you become a master of building trust. This book will explore these seven major factors, called Trust Cues, and give you strategies and tips on how to apply them in your own life to dramatically increase the trust you foster with other people.

The Seven Trust Cues	
Past Experience	Your track record of behavior that directly influences perceived trustworthiness
Credibility	Your believability built out of authenticity and expertise
Authenticity	Your transparency around your intentions, actions, and who you are
Clarity	Your ability to be clearly and easily understood
Voice	*How* you say things
Empathy	Your capacity to share another's feelings
Commonalities	Your shared experiences with others

When you understand the role each factor plays in creating connections with others and begin employing them in your conversations and presentations, you will increase your impact and the influence of your message, whatever it may be.

The rest of this book is organized around these seven factors. Chapters 3 through 9 will dive into each factor's importance in the trust-building process and give you simple strategies to increase trust in your presentations and conversations by leveraging that factor. Chapter 10 will cover everything you need to understand to present to large audiences. Knowing how to leverage these seven factors to quickly build and maintain trust with your audience is a game-changer.

I hope to accomplish two goals with this book. The first is awareness. I want you to be aware of the factors that create trust. Once you are aware of the seven trust factors, you will begin to recognize them in your daily life as you encounter other people and either trust or don't trust them. You'll immediately begin to see things you never saw before and say things to yourself like "That's why I don't trust this person," or "I immediately trusted this person, and now I know what they did to create that."

My second goal is that you will become more effective in helping other people trust *you*, whether you are speaking to large audiences or mostly in one-on-one conversations. Ensuring that the people you are speaking to trust you is an important part of communication. Adjusting the things you are doing (or not doing) in a conversation to create trust is a key part of that process. Once you learn the seven factors of trust and how to adjust what you can do to affect them, you will be able to create trust in any situation, large or small.

In a world rife with miscommunication and distrust, caring about how we connect and communicate with others and learning how to build trust with one another is the first step to building a better world. This isn't impossible; we can all learn to be better communicators. But it does take a certain amount of compassion and a desire to improve the lives of those around us. Whether you have an uplifting message to share or a product or service that can make someone's life better, you'll leave a lasting impression when you have the trust of another person.

CHAPTER 2

The Hidden Cost of Bad Communication

Think back to the first speech you ever gave. It was probably a book report or something similar that you had to research, write about, and then present to your class. When we learn this process in school, our goal is to just get in and out as soon as possible—or at least not make fools of ourselves.

Moreover, Johnny over there in the far back corner probably doesn't care about the habitats of iguanas. He just wants to keep doodling on his desk while your presentation takes up the teacher's attention. So as you were writing and creating posterboards, you weren't thinking about the most logical layout for the information or how the audience would best receive what you were trying to say. You were just trying not to fail.

Unless you take a speech class in college or have a great English teacher, you may never actually learn that there is a science to creating a compelling presentation. And you may be surprised to learn that we mess up presentations all the time by not putting the right information in the right place.

Further, you may not realize that every conversation you have is a mini-presentation. If you're on the sales floor, at the head of a classroom, wearing a stethoscope, or dressed in a uniform, every interaction with another person is an opportunity to create the trust needed to ensure better outcomes for all. That could be convincing the patient to take their medication or purchasing the warranty for a washing machine. But all too often, we lose trust little by little because we are simply not aware of what actually builds (or destroys) trust.

Lost Trust Equals Lost Opportunities

A bad presentation is a bad conversation, and no one wants to be stuck in one of those. In a bad conversation, the speaker is not aware of their body language, the delivery of what they're actually saying, or even the content of the conversation. They may mumble, speak too fast, or avoid eye contact. They might jump from one topic to the next or try to steer the conversation in a certain direction. They may suck up all of someone's time and miss certain cues, like someone checking their phone or watch. Similarly, a bad presenter is not conscious of his or her audience, fails to practice their presentation, isn't organized, or doesn't speak clearly. You get the idea.

I don't believe anyone intentionally sets out to give a bad presentation or a terrible conversation. Sometimes it just happens. We might be scared or worried; we may run out of time to prepare; we may be trying to impress and say things we don't really mean. Or we might be new to the experience of presenting (or selling or working with customers). Whatever the reason, when we don't present well, we lose trust with our audience. When we lose trust with our audience, we lose our chance to impact them with our message.

That may sound a bit over the top, but every time you speak, whether it's to one person or a thousand people, you are trying to convey a message. In conversation, it may be something spontaneous in response to the other person, but you have a message all the same. And yet if you don't have the other person's trust, you might as well be speaking to the wall.

Trust is a difficult thing to define, but we know what it feels like and that it's a vital and foundational piece of relationships— and everything is built on relationships. Trust creates feelings of safety and enhances our ability to get along, which reduces conflict. It allows us to be vulnerable. When there's trust in a relationship, we believe the other person and believe *in* them as well. We're willing to follow leaders we trust. We're willing to accept advice from trusted confidantes. Trust runs the world. So when it's broken or when it's not established at all, that's a problem for everyone.

That's where the Trust Cues come in. When you know and cultivate your ability to engage the seven Trust Cues, you increase your trust with your audience, which leads to better outcomes.

Cultivating Trust

In Chapter 1, we established that the Trust Cues include Past Experiences, Credibility, Authenticity, Clarity, Voice, Empathy, and Commonalities. Not only do these cues build trust, but they also create a compelling presentation and influence the fluctuations of trust levels in a positive way. When you put the right information in the right place, trust naturally grows.

Trust is typically lowest at the beginning when the audience has no past experience with the speaker and limited knowledge about them. So in the opening of a presentation, if you share a personal story that resonates with the audience (think Authenticity, Empathy, and Commonalities), trust levels tend to increase. As you progress through the opening, building stronger connections, trust continues to rise. When the presentation transitions to the core content, the "meat and potatoes," trust levels can further increase if the information is perceived as helpful and addresses the audience's problems or answers their key questions (Clarity and Credibility). The highest point of trust in the entire presentation usually occurs at the end of the content delivery, right before the call to action.

Once you initiate the call to action, the audience recognizes a shift in the type of communication. The personal stories and content pave the way for a persuasive attempt to encourage action, whether it's a direct sales pitch, a request to take a next step, or even an offer of something free. This transition can trigger an immediate drop in trust levels. Suddenly, you're asking the audience to participate in some way, to put some skin in the game, to reciprocate in this newly formed relationship. Yet as trust was likely high just before the call to action, you still benefit from this established rapport.

Structuring your presentation with an engaging opening story and helpful content prior to the call to action is crucial for maximizing trust. Presentations that begin with an offer, sales pitches that rush to the sale, or conversations that are overtly sales-oriented from the outset often miss this opportunity to build trust through connection and assistance before asking for something. It's normal for trust to dip when you first make your offer. That's why cultivating sufficient trust beforehand will help you navigate this phase more effectively.

When you believe what you're saying and say it with conviction, speak at the right speed, and say it loud enough for the audience to actually hear it, you exponentially increase your effectiveness. That's how voice plays into it.

In the coming chapters, I'll take you through each of the seven Trust Cues and show you how to use them to create compelling presentations and have effective conversations.

It is possible to build trust and build it quickly. It is possible to design better pitches and presentations, and you don't have to go back to school to learn how. It is possible to speak your message in a way that engages people and results in your desired outcomes. Trust me.

Now let's begin.

CHAPTER 3

Trust Cue #1: Past Experiences

I'd had a long day teaching a workshop about giving effective presentations, and the only thought getting me through that last hour was the meal I planned to have at my favorite restaurant. I walked into the restaurant and immediately felt my shoulders relax. The smell of baking bread and grilled steak wafted through the dining room and greeted me at the host station.

The hostess on duty greeted me and led me to a small table. As she set down the menu, I almost told her I didn't need it; I already knew I wanted a medium rare filet with a salad and mashed potatoes. Simple—and simply wonderful. But I accepted the menu anyway out of habit. When the waiter came by, we exchanged the usual pleasantries. I let him run through the specials, even though I had already made my decision.

While he grabbed my water, I flipped through the menu. My eyes landed on the meal I'd been craving all day. I could almost taste it as I placed my order. Waiting for the food only increased my anticipation of that first bite. When the food finally arrived, I lit up. It was the moment I'd been waiting for.

I sliced off a piece of seared steak and began to chew.

And my daydreams of the perfect meal evaporated.

Something was off.

A flicker of disappointment crossed my face. This wasn't what I anticipated. I'd been here countless times before and never had a single complaint. But tonight, the food just wasn't as good. I still don't quite know if it was the seasoning, the cook, the atmosphere at the restaurant that night, or something completely different, but I left feeling let down, not entirely discouraged but not satisfied either. Even still, I knew I'd be back. One bad visit wouldn't cancel out the many good ones I'd had before.

The same thought process applies to our interpersonal relationships. One of the most significant determinants of trust is an individual's past experiences. When someone in your life consistently demonstrates honesty and trustworthiness, you develop a strong sense of reliance on them. Trust is not a one-time event but an accumulation of consistently kept promises.

This consistent reliability also shapes expectations for future interactions. Once trust is established, less effort is required to maintain it. A history of reliability enhances predictability and reduces uncertainty for others, strengthening trust in both your personal and professional relationships. Our world is always changing. The minute we grow comfortable with something, it can suddenly shift. In times like these, we gravitate toward those who consistently demonstrate trustworthiness, whose word is their bond, and who reliably fulfill their promises.

In contrast, a pattern of broken commitments or dishonesty creates distrust. One instance of dishonesty from a typically honest person might be met with understanding because they've earned the benefit of the doubt through past behavior. However, if someone with a history of unreliability fulfills a commitment, then it's seen as an exception, not a reflection of a fundamental change in their trustworthiness. In our minds, past behavior is a strong predictor of future trustworthiness. When a person has been unreliable, overcoming that is incredibly challenging. They have to be nearly flawless in everything they do because even one mistake can reinforce the perception that they're unreliable. Trust is not a one-time event but an accumulation of consistently kept promises.

Promises Are Commitments
Waiting to Be Fulfilled

It might sound simple to keep the promises we make, but in practice, it can be the hardest thing to do. For example, when checking your email first thing in the morning, you might respond to a colleague that you'll have the numbers for their report by lunch. You promise. But then right after hitting send, your boss pulls you into a meeting that lasts well past lunch, pushing all thoughts about your colleague and your promise out of your head. Now all you can think about is grabbing a quick sandwich and getting your boss what they need based on the hours-long meeting you just had.

That is fine if it happens once. You can make it up to your colleague. But if it happens more often than not, they'll stop asking for your help because they won't believe your word. The same thing happens every time you forget to call a customer back, fail to follow up with a patient, or start a presentation saying you'll talk about x, y, and z and then never get to those points. Broken promises create broken trust and erode relationships.

How to Create Positive (Past) Experiences

This is all well and good, you might be thinking, *but what happens when there are no past experiences to rely on?* How can you quickly cultivate trust the first time you meet someone or, in the case of presentations, as a speaker?

We're all human. We know that we're not made to be perfect, but we can be mindful of the promises or commitments we make. That's why it's important to create a margin for error while also taking ownership when you fall short. Here are concrete steps you can take to build trust.

Make Small Promises Early: Early in a conversation with someone, intentionally make small, easy-to-fulfill promises, and then quickly deliver on them. You could start this process even before the conversation begins with something like, "Let's meet at 3:00 p.m. I'll make a reservation for us to hold a table," and then, when you show up at 3:00 p.m. and have a reservation for a table waiting, you've easily fulfilled two promises. If you say something like, "I'll bring these documents with me to the meeting," then actually bring them. Promise made and kept.

During a conversation, you can also make specific, easily fulfilled commitments about the conversation itself. "I have forty minutes set aside for this conversation. Let's use our time wisely during these forty minutes,""and then finish the meeting in forty minutes. "I'm not going to waste your time here today. I'm going to give you concrete deliverables that you can take action on," and then actually deliver concrete deliverables. "After this meeting, I will send you additional information." Be sure to send it. "Let's connect tomorrow to schedule our next meeting," and then actually connect.

Intentionally have a number of small, easy-to-fulfill promises ready to go early in a conversation so you can quickly establish a reliable track record with the person you're talking to through consistent experiences of you fulfilling your promises.

Always Follow Through on Your Promises: As your relationship develops, dedicate yourself to continuing to fulfill your commitments. Many of us have felt the pressure to overpromise, even when we have doubts about following through. Instead, continue to focus on making small, achievable commitments consistently. This further builds rapport and reinforces trust.

When meeting with a client, if you say you'll call them when a particular product comes in, make sure you call them when that product comes in. When you're leading a team and announce a meeting will last thirty minutes, adhere to that time frame. Even seemingly minor commitments can be valuable for building trust. That is similar to taking out small loans and repaying them promptly or using a line of credit in small increments and paying on time. Those actions are taken to build a positive credit history.

By consistently fulfilling small commitments, you demonstrate your trustworthiness. You show others that you honor your word. People will logically infer that if you are reliable with small matters, you are likely to be reliable with larger, more significant commitments.

In contrast, failing to follow through on small promises can erode confidence in your ability to handle larger responsibilities. Your audience will be more inclined to trust your offers and claims if your teaching and information are consistently reliable.

Clearly Document Your Commitments: A fulfilled commitment that goes unnoticed has limited impact. It may seem boastful to highlight how you've consistently kept your word, but doing so is a powerful way to build trust. Make it a habit to record your commitments and later note when they are fulfilled.

Let's say you're addressing an audience. Start by outlining the topics you plan to cover. After guiding them through each point, conclude the presentation by confirming that you delivered on everything you promised at the beginning. It's as easy as saying, "To recap, we discussed . . ." and continue from there.

For salespeople, whenever you schedule a follow-up call, start with an opening statement like, "I wanted to check in *as promised* and share the next steps with you." That shows your client that you are dependable, which gives you a better chance to close the sale.

Each instance reinforces your reliability and builds credibility. Failing to acknowledge your fulfilled commitments is a missed opportunity to strengthen trust.

Regularly Check In to Confirm Satisfaction: Silence doesn't always indicate satisfaction. Let's look at it from a manager's perspective. Imagine you're onboarding a new hire. You assure them your team values safety and inclusion. A few weeks pass and you hear no complaints, so you assume everything is going well. But then the turnover rate starts to rise out of nowhere. That could be a sign of underlying dissatisfaction. To fulfill your promise of safety and inclusion, schedule regular check-ins and ask clear questions to actively gather feedback on the perceived level of safety and inclusion. Emphasize that you are following up because it is a commitment you made and its fulfillment is important to you.

This proactive approach fulfills two commitments: the initial promise and the commitment to follow up, which can significantly enhance trust. Similarly, during a presentation, after covering the promised topics, don't just state that you have done so; ask the audience if their questions have been answered and if they feel the topics were adequately addressed. Their affirmative response reinforces the perception of your reliability.

Address Misunderstandings Promptly: Sometimes, it's not that you failed to deliver. It could be a simple matter of miscommunication. Many of us have experienced situations where we believed a commitment was fulfilled, but the other person saw it differently. In these moments, ask them what their understanding of the commitment was and where they believe it fell short. Listen with empathy and respond without defensiveness. Then, explain your own understanding of the situation. Oftentimes, the issue comes down to a misunderstanding. Acknowledge any shortcomings in your communication, emphasizing your sincere intent to communicate effectively.

In these situations, having the right intentions makes a significant difference. Owning your mistakes, admitting when you have fallen short, and honestly addressing miscommunications while actively working to improve future communication will significantly advance the trust-building process.

Acknowledge Your Shortcomings Transparently: If, for some reason, you have previously missed a commitment or not followed through on a promise that you made, acknowledge it up front and clearly explain how you have improved or adjusted. You do not need to spend a lot of time making excuses or giving reasons why you did not follow through.

Own the mistake, and focus your explanations on clearly explaining how you have made changes, adjusted systems, or improved yourself so it doesn't happen again. This is the way to overcome someone's experience of you being someone who does not fulfill their commitments.

If you highlight your past track record of keeping your promises, lay down some easy-to-fulfill promises and then fulfill them, and acknowledge any shortcomings transparently during the conversation, the person you're talking to will be able to trust you more because their experience of you is someone who consistently and reliably fulfills their promises.

Whether you are beginning to build a relationship with one person or trying to connect with an audience from the stage, create opportunities for small commitments that you can quickly fulfill in order to establish trust through experiences. As you do this over and over, these promises kept will form a strong foundation for future interactions. You'll become the speaker everyone wants to book and see; you'll become the salesperson everyone wants to work with; you'll become the team member everyone requests for their team. Your word is your bond, no matter how small, so take care what you say.

Creating Trust Activity

At the end of every Trust Cue chapter, there will be a short activity to give you a chance to work the Trust Cue into your process. If you consistently practice each Trust Cue, by the time you finish reading, you'll be well on your way to transforming your relationships and creating the kind of impact you desire.

For this first activity, choose two of the concrete steps above to practice today. In your journal or electronic notes, write down which ones they are, and then, when you've completed them, document *how* you completed them. Keeping track of your successes will not only reinforce the behavior, but it will also remind you that you can follow through on promises you make to yourself.

CHAPTER 4

Trust Cue #2: Credibility

Imagine that your primary care doctor retired, and you had to establish yourself with a new provider. You ask friends and family for a recommendation, but none of those doctors are accepting new patients. With no better options, you decide to try the young guy, fresh out of medical school, who replaced your physician.

You walk into the familiar office and sit down on the examination table, ready to meet the person charged with your medical care. The first thing you notice is the new decor, including a freshly hung diploma on the wall. It's slightly askew, so you straighten it, but as you adjust the frame, you read the name of the medical school, and don't recognize it. That's fine, you don't know the name of every school, but you also see that the ink is slightly smeared and printing quality is dingy. No matter. The piece of paper doesn't have to be perfect as long as the doctor is good.

The door opens and the doctor rushes in, glasses on the tip of his nose, hair mussed, button-down shirt wrinkly, and credentials stuffed into his front shirt pocket instead of clipped on. He closes the door and puts on the white lab coat waiting for him. You notice a tiny drop of brownish red, which you hope is ketchup, near the hem of the coat. You're less impressed at this point, but the office hired him, so he's probably fine.

Then he asks you about your family medical history. You name off a few conditions. He writes them down. But before you can continue, he holds up a hand and says, "How do you spell that last one?"

How do you feel about this doctor's qualifications now? Still want to give him the benefit of the doubt, or has he failed to establish credibility with you? I'd suggest you thank him for his time, but you want to go in a different direction—right out the door and back to your car in the parking lot.

Credibility boils down to whether or not your audience believes you are a reliable and knowledgeable source of information. As you just experienced, several factors shape how others perceive someone's credibility—and sometimes it's as simple as the circumstances.

Establishing credibility strengthens your message by reinforcing both authenticity and expertise. The specific factors determining credibility can vary depending on the industry. Sometimes, outward signs play a role.

Displaying degrees, certifications, or licenses can serve as external indicators of your expertise. (Just make sure the ink isn't smeared.) Diplomas from reputable universities displayed on the wall give someone more confidence in your ability. People are more inclined to believe a message when it comes from a source they view as credible, giving them greater confidence in the information shared.

Dressing the part also can enhance your credibility. For example, medical professionals who wear a white lab coat and stethoscope are often perceived as more credible. If you want people to believe in you, put your best foot forward. Comb your hair, iron your shirt, and spot-treat stains.

A strong reputation also significantly contributes to credibility. It's important to understand the difference between reputation and past experiences. In the last chapter, we said that past experiences are your *direct* interactions with a person, business, or organization. Reputation, on the other hand, is based on what you *hear* about their interactions with others. Someone might have a negative reputation, yet all your personal experiences with them have been positive. Conversely, someone with a stellar reputation might have provided you with less-than-ideal experiences. While distinct, both reputation and past experiences contribute to overall trustworthiness.

Why does this matter? A credible speaker is more likely to influence the audience's decisions, and for sustained professional success, building and maintaining credibility is absolutely vital.

Don't Let Your Credibility Crumble

Everything you've read so far on credibility seems like common sense, right? It seems like the kinds of things you learned in elementary school. But in the age of technology and social media, credibility is becoming harder and harder to establish and maintain. One bad review, one post that people don't like, one question about your alma mater—all that can potentially tank your credibility with someone.

I'm not saying you need to be the most benign person ever. No, quite the opposite. As you may have learned back in school, not everyone will like you, and that's okay. The key is creating and maintaining credibility with the people you *want* to reach.

In other words, who is your target audience? Or who are you presenting to? What is important to them? And what do they need to know about you in order to nail that all-important first impression? This is something you can think about whether you're meeting with a new client one on one, speaking to a large group, or creating business-to-client-facing marketing materials.

Of course, keep in mind that you won't be talking to your target audience every time in every setting. But you can always ask these questions and tailor your presentation or conversational points to highlight the things that will establish your credibility.

How to Establish Credibility

Beyond putting on a clean shirt and carrying around your framed diploma, there are plenty of ways to establish credibility.

Obtain and Clearly Communicate Relevant Qualifications: The first step is identifying what your audience considers to be relevant qualifications in your field. Remember, what's relevant varies by industry.

Once you determine this, there are several ways to showcase your credentials: a framed degree on the wall, a seal in the corner of a website or email signature, or highlighting certifications and licenses in your bio. These small signals speak before you even say a word.

Even adding a few relevant initials after your name or casually mentioning relevant credentials near the beginning of a formal presentation is a great way to establish your credibility. While you can mention these qualifications yourself, it's often more impactful when the person introducing you highlights them instead.

For instance, in the early part of a conversation, when you are making small talk or getting to know the other person, you could tell a story about a time you were in training or in school, earning a degree, a credential, or a license. You could tell a story about working with another client, and name-drop someone the person knows or has a previous relationship with. If you set aside time to drop your credentials, it will appear that you are boasting. If you do it early in the conversation while you're telling other stories and catching up on other topics, it will appear more natural and more humble.

Provide Evidence of Past Successes

When communicating with others, find ways to weave your past successes throughout the conversation. The best way to do this is storytelling, often referred to as testimonials. I call them examples, case studies, or proof that the methods or information I'm sharing actually work.

I once worked with a successful financial advisor who regularly gave presentations to couples preparing for retirement. He spoke in detail about tax planning and income strategies, but he never mentioned the number of people he had actually helped. When I asked, he told me he had helped over 400 families retire successfully and remain financially secure throughout their retirement years. That's the kind of information your audience needs and wants to hear. This kind of information helps people understand the real impact of what you do.

Choose Your Timing

What matters more than the story is the timing of when it's told. Whatever you do, avoid sharing these successes during your call to action. So many speakers and salespeople save their stories for the end of their presentation when they ask the audience to buy something or take a specific action. Let me tell you why that is less impactful.

The human brain is wired to categorize different types of communication. We can discern between storytelling, teaching, and selling. People typically don't take notes during stories, but they do when content is being taught. An audience's trust level is generally higher when they perceive you as an educator rather than a salesperson. Hence the most effective time to share your examples of past successes is when you are teaching content.

We've all experienced conversations that initially seemed friendly only to realize a sales agenda was at play. It starts out with a friendly smile that progresses to a seemingly organic conversation. And then the shoe drops, and they're introducing you to a new product or business opportunity. The realization that you're being sold on something shifts your perception of the entire interaction, triggering skepticism.

Believing we're being taught helps us listen with more trust and a greater willingness to learn and act on the information. That's why it's more effective to share your proof of past successes— stories, examples, testimonials, or case studies— while teaching content rather than during a sales pitch.

Leverage Endorsements from Reputable Sources: As you achieve success, actively seek endorsements from those you have worked with. Think about how brands build instant credibility. When a well-known athlete or celebrity endorses a product, people are more likely to trust it and become more open to trying it, simply because someone they admire stands behind the brand.

As you grow, aim to recruit some clients with greater name recognition to enhance the credibility of your endorsements and stories. The more respected the client or the success story, the greater its impact.

If you have worked with someone well-known in your industry or among your audience, don't hesitate to highlight that connection. Leveraging their endorsement can help build trust and credibility with future clients. Testimonies can take many forms. Written quotes, audio clips, and videos can be shared across different social media platforms, presentations, or even in one-on-one conversations.

Early in your career or business, you might not have high-profile success stories to rely on, and that's completely normal.

Most of your initial clients or case studies might be individuals or entities unknown to a wider audience. Even testimonials from lesser known clients can reinforce your credibility, and over time, the small wins will build a powerful foundation of trust.

Casually Reference a Third Party: Another way to build credibility is to casually reference a third party—a reputable source or an individual who trusts your expertise to indirectly validate your credibility. As human beings, we associate people whose names are mentioned close together. Sometimes, just mentioning that you were working with someone, or just mentioning that you were reading someone else's book, can attach your name to their name and increase your credibility.

In the best-case scenario, your third-party reference would be someone who has relationships with both you and the other person in the conversation, or someone who is so well-known that you're quite certain the person you are talking to knows who that person is. You could say, for instance, "I was talking to so-and-so the other day, who told me how much this information helped them in their life." That third-party reference, using someone the other person trusts and knows, will build your credibility and their trust in you.

Demonstrate Continuous Learning and Improvement: When was the last time you explored new insights in your industry? Have you read something relevant lately, taken a course, or attended an event? Staying informed about cutting-edge developments, current topics, and emerging trends gives your credibility a noticeable boost. How you communicate this ongoing learning process is vital to your credibility. Continuously stay at the forefront of knowledge in your specific field.

However, saying outright that you're the most knowledgeable can sound arrogant, and you don't want that. A better approach is to share stories about your experience attending industry events, engaging with experts, participating in discussions on current trends, and experimenting with new strategies. Framing your experience this way shows that you recognize the limits of their knowledge and are proactive in staying current with industry advancements.

Back when I used to help schools identify students for special education programs, the legal and research landscape was rapidly changing. Instead of just presenting the latest best practices, I shared my journey by saying things like this: "We used to believe this was the best way to serve students, but recent research and our practical experience have shown us a better approach. Now, we serve students this way, and here are the improved outcomes we are seeing."

By illustrating how your thinking has evolved rather than presenting one "right" way, you demonstrate continuous learning and a commitment to improvement. That makes all your information, both established and newly acquired, more credible because the audience sees you as someone open to adapting based on new evidence and best practices.

Imagine a car salesperson walking you through the evolution of headlight technology. They explain how a once-popular model type had been replaced by a newer, safer, and more widely preferred design based on recent research and customer feedback. As a customer, you're more inclined to consider the updated model because it feels like you've gained an insider's perspective on both options. This shows that the salesperson's recommendation is based on current advancements, not just what's available for purchase. And that builds credibility.

These are valuable experiences to share on social meda or during speaking engagements, sales conversations, and other interactions. Doing so signals to your audience that your information is up-to-date, factually sound, and therefore credible.

Provide Immediate Value: A final step in establishing credibility is to provide immediate value. Offer one or two practical insights on the main topic or problem, making sure these practical insights are relevant to the needs of your audience. The earlier you do that in your conversation— shortly after the connection portion of the conversation and early in the content or meat of the conversation—the longer it will pay off.

Watch the body language of your conversational companion or individuals in the audience for signals that the tips you've given them were insightful and relevant to their needs. If you are getting positive body language signals—nodding heads, leaning in, things like that—continue down this road of offering insights. If you are not receiving positive body language signals, back off this line of strategy and advice, and look for another opportunity to meet their needs in a relevant way.

The longer you're in the business, the more your credibility can and will build, especially if you are intentional about following the steps described above. If you find yourself stagnating, reevaluate. Ask yourself about the last time *you* went through training or learned something new about your industry. When was the last time you updated your website or presentation? Who was the last connection you made, and have you kept in touch with them? It's not always easy to find time to continue to build your credibility, but it will always be worth it.

Creating Trust Activity

Before you move on to the next chapter, I want to give you a quick list of questions to answer about building your credibility. There's no need to write down your answers, but if you haven't guessed it yet, we're going to use those answers to build out your Must-Do list.

- **Communicating Your Qualifications**

  o Does your website, email signature, and presentation have your credentials and qualifications listed?

  o Do you have a framed degree on your office wall?

  o Do you have your qualifications noted, even briefly, in your bio—whether on your website or in the intro copy used before you present?

- **Past Successes**

  o Do you have testimonials or the number of clients served noted on your website or in your presentations or marketing materials?

  o Do you have a system in place to gather this information, something like a post-service survey?

- **Making Connections**

  o Do you have relationships with other people in your industry, well-known or otherwise?

  o Do you have testimonials or quotes from them regarding your credibility or how you helped them?

  o Do you keep up with the people you meet at industry events?

- **Continuous Learning**

  o When was the last time you took a class or a training, or learned something new in your industry?

- Is this something you do on a regular basis or only once in a while?

o Do you ever bring it up in presentations or in conversations?

- **Provide Immediate Value**

o Do you offer any solutions to your audience or clients during presentations?

- If so, are they giving you positive or negative feedback? (If it's negative feedback, make sure you're giving the right presentation to the right audience. That could quickly solve the feedback problem. I know it sounds obvious, but so are door signs that read "Pull," and yet we all still push when we try to enter.)

If you answered yes to a particular question, Great! You're taking the small yet important steps necessary to establish and build your credibility.

If you answered no to a question, add it as an action item to your Must-Do list. For example, if you said, "No, I don't keep up with people I meet at industry events. In fact, I don't even go to industry events!" then write down "1. Go to at least one industry event in the next year. 2. Meet at least one person. 3. Set a calendar reminder to email or call them once a quarter."

Taking these small but actionable steps to build your credibility will positively impact your relationship with your audience or customers.

CHAPTER 5

Trust Cue #3: Authenticity

I remember sitting through a well-known business executive's presentation at a leadership summit. She walked on stage in a sharp blazer, smiling confidently as the spotlight hit. Her slides were flawless—clean graphics, well-timed animations, even a few clever jokes that got polite laughs. Every sentence was polished and every gesture rehearsed like she had practiced in front of a mirror a hundred times. And based on who she was and the topic of her talk, I know she'd done this or a similar presentation before.

But about ten minutes in, I realized I was more focused on the lighting than her words. It all felt too perfect, like she was delivering a TED Talk to a camera, not speaking to real people. Yes, she was making eye contact with the audience, but even that felt highly rehearsed, like she was keeping a timer in her head and thought, *Every thirty seconds, look down.*

I kept waiting for a moment of spontaneity, a glimpse of who she *really* was—but it never came. By the end, I applauded out of politeness. I knew she'd nailed it, but I felt oddly untouched, unaffected by what I'd just learned.

When a presentation feels too rehearsed or too perfect, it creates distance with the audience. It becomes hard to connect on a person-to-person level. Yet I've learned that often, speakers focus so much on how they want to be perceived that they forget something more powerful—being themselves. Vulnerability and sincerity are more powerful than a flawless presentation.

Each of us operates from a set of core values and beliefs. Those values shape our decisions, guide our behavior, and influence how others experience us. When your behavior consistently aligns with those values and how your audience already perceives you, you establish credibility. That alignment is the foundation of authenticity.

Authenticity is not about perfection. It is about being grounded in who you are and showing up in a way that confirms what people already trust about you.

It also involves being transparent about your intentions and actions. When people understand your "why," it removes suspicion and builds clarity. Relatability plays a role too. When others see parts of themselves in you, they are more likely to engage openly and build mutual trust. This relatability encourages open communication and builds trust in both directions.

Whether you are delivering a formal presentation, engaging in a one-on-one conversation, or giving a sales pitch, being perceived as authentic and transparent is a vital factor in establishing trust. Your authenticity stands out most when you're consistent. Consistent behavior reinforces reliability, and reliability, in turn, strengthens authenticity.

People trust those who act predictably and in accordance with their stated values. Inconsistencies between your words and actions will negatively impact both your authenticity and your audience's level of trust in you. Authenticity is also demonstrated through commitment to moral and ethical standards. When your behavior and principles align, it reinforces trust through consistent and credible actions.

When We're Authentically Inauthentic

When I switched careers from teaching math to coaching speakers, I felt like I had a lot to prove. I had to show up and give perfect talks in order to demonstrate my credibility. I had to follow my script, my painstakingly crafted script, in order to capture my audience. And I had to practice my facial expressions and hand movements in front of a mirror to make sure I gave the right amount of emotion and engagement.

But do you know what I didn't anticipate? Audience *dis*-engagement.

In the last chapter I talked about how an audience will give you positive body language when they believe you. In those early presentations, I followed the Speakers Rulebook 101 to a tee, and as a result, I came across as genuinely inauthentic. I wasn't getting head nods; I was getting heads nodding off. I couldn't figure out what was going wrong.

Every person I asked said the same thing: "You're doing everything right."

You're doing everything right.

So why wasn't everything right?

Flustered and frustrated, I continued to book events and give the talk, changing a slide and commentary here, changing a slide and hand movement there. Nothing worked.

At the end of one of the longest weeks of my early speaking career, I had one presentation standing between me and the weekend I desperately needed. It was a Friday afternoon during the summer, and I'd worn my usual blue suit with a white, button-down, long-sleeved shirt (no tie) and stood in the glare of the hottest lights I'd ever encountered. The longer I spoke, the more I sweated. I could see on the faces of the audience that they were just as hot and bored with my presentation as I was. So I did the thing I wasn't supposed to do, and I went rogue.

I put my hand up to shield my eyes from the lights and talked to the lighting person in the back of the auditorium.

"Hey, can we turn down these stage lights for a minute and bring up the house lights?" They complied. And as the lights came up, I could see that the audience was confused. *Had the presentation ended and they didn't realize it?*

So I addressed the room: "It's hot in here, right? Those lights were killing me, so I thought we could turn them off. I know it's hard to see the presentation now, though, so I'll send a copy of the slide show to your managers, and they can get you a copy if you really want it. And if you don't mind, I'm going to take off this jacket and roll up my sleeves. Feel free to do the same."

I do not exaggerate when I tell you how relieved everyone looked, including me. While I continued to use the slides for myself, I didn't worry about the hand gestures and eye contact, and I let everything move forward as naturally as I could. In fact, I pretended that I was giving this talk to a group of friends and even dropped in some jokes. It turned out so great that I was invited back the following year.

When it comes to making connections and being vulnerable and sincere, I'm not saying to put typos in your slides, and I'm not saying don't rehearse. But leave room to be human because remember, you're speaking to humans. If you feel and sound like a robot, your audience will think you're a robot.

How to Be More *You*

There are many ways to enhance your audience's perception of your authenticity and create better connections. And you don't have to take off your jacket to do it.

Does Your Story Make Sense? We all have an origin story explaining how we arrived at our present point. Sometimes these steps resonate with our audience, and sometimes they don't. Does your narrative pass the "smell test"? Does it feel believable and logical?

Once I was speaking with a day trader who claimed he consistently made $10,000 a day trading stocks, yet he was selling a $500 online course on stock trading. I paused for a moment. If he truly had a method that generated that kind of daily income, why sell a low-cost course to begin with? It didn't add up, and that disconnect raised questions about his credibility.

Another time, I encountered a health professional who claimed her recovery from various ailments, including chronic conditions, was attributed solely to eliminating one food from her diet. The explanation felt incomplete as it didn't account for the potential complexity of her health issues.

You've probably experienced network marketers who simultaneously promote health products and a business opportunity. People often don't perceive these two areas as inherently linked, making it difficult to believe that one solution can effectively address both. While the individual's experience might be genuine, the narrative can lack authenticity and seem unconvincing.

Network marketers often find more success by focusing either on selling their products or promoting the business opportunity—not trying to do both simultaneously. That makes their story more coherent and their offer more authentic.

Self-Reflection and Beliefs

Regularly examining your personal values and beliefs is a powerful way to enhance your authenticity and transparency. I encourage you to focus on two things. First, assess whether your actions consistently reflect the core principles you live by. Second, consider how well those principles are integrated into your communication.

For example, if your faith is a significant part of your life and business, your actions should clearly reflect those beliefs. You can also weave them into your message, whether you're giving a formal presentation or speaking casually with a person one-on-one.

One of the most effective places to subtly demonstrate your values is in your opening story. This first impression sets the tone and gives your audience a glimpse of what really drives you. The story itself doesn't need to be about your faith. Even a simple reference such as "We did this on our way home from church one day" can convey this aspect of your identity.

You can also integrate your core beliefs into your presentations through an "I believe" statement. That kind of statement is just a bridge that connects your personal experience to your teaching expertise. It looks like this: Your personal experiences create your beliefs; your beliefs give you the passion to teach people what you have learned. Every presentation should include a concise sentence that reveals your fundamental conviction related to your topic. If I were to sum mine up in an "I believe" statement, it would be this: "I believe that trust is the most critical factor in whether an audience listens and responds favorably to your communication." Or "I believe that your voice is your most powerful marketing tool; the growth of any endeavor hinges primarily on how you articulate its value." You can take it even further for the audience by giving a bit of the story around how you learned this or what your personal experience with it is.

To provide more context for your message, share your "I believe" statement early in your presentation. Ideally, say it right after your opening story. In everyday conversations, say it after the initial pleasantries but before transitioning into the main topic. That helps set the stage for the discussion.

Open Communication: Mutual trust is built through your willingness to share your thoughts and feelings, along with encouraging reciprocal openness. A sales conversation should always be a two-way exchange, not a monologue. So when you talk about yourself, avoid presenting only a highlight reel of successes. Share a balanced view, including both your strengths and weaknesses, what you know, and what you are still learning.

A telltale sign of inauthenticity is an immediate response the moment someone finishes speaking. This often signals a lack of genuine listening. You can foster reciprocal openness by being an active listener. Have you ever been in a conversation where it was clear the other person was listening just to respond, not to understand? Or maybe you found yourself unable to get a word in because the other person never left space for you to speak?

Most of us have experienced that at some point. When it happens, it can leave you feeling overlooked, like your input doesn't matter. You might even notice yourself becoming more guarded. These are the kind of reactions we want to avoid, especially when we're trying to build trust with someone in a one-on-one conversation.

Even something as simple as a brief pause before responding shows that you've thoughtfully considered the other person's words. On the other hand, jumping in too quickly or interrupting signals a lack of authentic, two-way communication.

Admit Mistakes: I toured a house with a real estate agent who was only highlighting its best features. Everything sounded great but almost *too* great. It wasn't until I asked about the number of bedrooms that she paused and said, "It has just two, but they're generously sized." That moment changed the entire conversation. Her honesty made the pitch more believable. No house is perfect, and acknowledging that didn't hurt the sale; it made her more trustworthy.

In my speaking career, I've addressed audiences of varying sizes, from a massive arena with 16,000 people to a small hotel ballroom with only five attendees. Sharing both these experiences creates a more relatable and authentic image. It shows that success isn't constant and that there are ups and downs. This balanced storytelling increases your perceived authenticity and transparency.

When sharing your own stories, avoid portraying yourself as perfect. If you are always the hero in every narrative, your audience will likely find it unbelievable. Share stories where you shine and stories where you stumble. A person who openly acknowledges errors and takes responsibility for them will always be perceived as more authentic and transparent than someone who portrays themselves as flawless. Demonstrating humility fosters trust. That is why sharing weaknesses, even minor ones, with your audience is so important.

Simple admissions like "Sometimes I get nervous when I speak," or "I'm a bit clumsy; I even spilled water on my shirt just before coming in," reveal your humanity. These small vulnerabilities show your audience that you are presenting your true, unfiltered self, not a polished facade.

Little admissions go a long way in building authenticity. Be transparent and vulnerable. Be the first one to share a weakness. Be the first one to be vulnerable. Share instances of forgetfulness, mistakes made, lessons learned, and recent minor corrections. If you are willing to talk about not just the things you are good at but the mistakes you have made and the areas where you are still trying to improve, your audience will respond in kind. The net result of this is increased trust and perception of authenticity.

Consistent Actions: When your behavior consistently aligns with your stated values, people take notice. One way to demonstrate this is by making it clear that you're willing to walk away from a sale if it compromises your values.

For example, you might say you wouldn't sell a product to someone if the product clearly isn't right for them. You wouldn't sell it to someone who would go into debt trying to afford it. In addition to being aligned with your beliefs, it's important to communicate these actions to your audience.

Try sharing a social media post about a recent interaction where you advised a prospect that your services weren't the best fit for their needs, even offering alternative suggestions. This level of transparency reinforces your commitment to your values and builds trust. Consistently acting on your values and sharing those instances—whether in formal presentations, sales conversations, or casual interactions—significantly enhances your perceived authenticity.

Seek Feedback: Actively encourage others to provide honest feedback, and then receive it with gratitude. Feedback is valuable because it helps improve and maintain your authenticity. Being defensive toward feedback can signal arrogance and an unwillingness to grow.

Embracing feedback and implementing changes demonstrate authenticity and a commitment to lifelong learning. Feedback not only refines your communication but also improves your practices, ensuring you remain at the forefront of your field.

I've met two kinds of people throughout my coaching career. One is the person who says they're very successful but makes it clear they're not open to any kind of feedback. That always makes me wonder how successful someone can really be if they're only willing to hear praise and not constructive input.

Then there are the others, like billionaires I've worked with, who ask me to "tear apart" their ideas and "give it to me straight" without sparing their feelings. If I had to choose who to trust, it would be the person who welcomes feedback. If you ask me, I truly believe that willingness to be corrected is a big part of why they've been so successful.

Audiences appreciate this vulnerability and willingness to learn since it fosters a sense of two-way communication and reinforces your authenticity and transparency. So, be open to sharing stories about how you previously approached things but have since adopted a different method based on feedback.

Sharing stories of improvement, acknowledging mistakes, and highlighting changes made based on feedback all contribute to the audience perceiving you as authentic. An opening story that presents a balanced view of your experiences—including strengths and weaknesses, avoiding the "hero" narrative, and incorporating stories of growth and adaptation—will lead your audience to see you as genuine and transparent, ultimately increasing their trust in you.

Align Your Words and Your Actions Immediately

Ensure that your body language and your tone match your verbal message. If you are talking about something sad or the person you're in a conversation with who has just shared something sad, you should slow your pace of speech, lower your volume, and lean in to the person you're talking to. Limit your gestures and your movement at that time.

On the other hand, if the person who you are talking to has just shared great news or you have just shared great news with the person you are speaking with, you should increase the volume of your speech, increase the pace of your speech, and increase your gestures and movement. That will align your words and your actions. Many times, the person we're speaking to does not appear to be authentic because they are out of alignment. Their body language, movement, and voice do not match the words they are saying or the emotions of the moment.

Be Present, Not Distracted: Your phone is your worst enemy when trying to be authentic. The distraction of looking at messages or waiting for another alert on our phone can make the person we're talking to feel like we're not present in the conversation. That goes a long way in hurting trust. Align your words and actions by silencing your phone and putting it away so you can be present with the person you are talking to.

Express Your Honest Intentions: During a conversation, if you are trying to get a specific outcome, the way to build trust is to let the person know you are in this conversation to get a specific outcome. Clearly articulate your sincere intentions for the conversation at the beginning of the conversation. Avoid making vague statements, and be specific about what you would like to achieve. If you are trying to persuade or convince the other person, let the other person know you are trying to persuade or convince them.

For example, I work with a lot of financial advisors who meet one on one with prospective clients. Some of them are coy and evasive about the purpose of the one-on-one meeting. But the best approach, and the one that has the highest conversion rate, is letting the prospect know about the purpose of the conversation early in the conversation: "Our meeting today is to get to know each other a bit better and see if it might be a good fit for us to work further together."

If you are seeking information, let the other person know you're seeking information. If you're just trying to catch up, let the other person know that your goal is just to catch up. When you are honest about your intentions in a conversation, there is a genuineness and a sincerity that breeds authenticity. Being transparent about these intentions will build trust.

Authenticity is an important part of the trust-building process in any one-on-one conversation. Don't be afraid to be vulnerable and show your weaknesses. Make sure your body language is in alignment with the moment and the words you are saying, and tell the other person your honest intentions for the conversation early. Then be true to those intentions. All these things will increase trust.

Creating Trust Activity

It's easy to fall into the trap of rehearsed perfection. We see it and hear it all the time in social media, interviews, and presentations. We all want to look good and exude confidence, but the key is doing so while also demonstrating our common humanity.

Before moving into the next chapter, pick two (or more) of the authenticity-building actions the next time you give a presentation or speak with a customer. Be sure to note the responses you get and see how it changes your ability to connect.

If you want to take it one step further, use one or more of these strategies in your social media posts. Try admitting to a mistake and tell how it affected you and what you learned. See how it changes your engagement. You'll be surprised by how relatable you'll suddenly become.

CHAPTER 6

Trust Cue #4: Clarity

It's a beautiful Monday morning. As I drive to the office, the sky is a deep, clear blue. The sun is shining. It's the perfect temperature to commute with your windows down and your favorite song playing on the radio. It couldn't be a better day. Then you sit down at your desk and start checking your email.

"Good work, team," your boss begins. "We've outperformed projections for the last two quarters even though across the industry, business is down. As a result, we're going to do some reorganization, right-size some teams, redistribute resources, and really buckle down. More to come in the meeting at 10 a.m."

What? We did better than expected. And right-size teams? What does that mean?

You hear your cubicle neighbors whispering about the email they also just read.

"I heard they're going to lay off all of Production East," one of them says.

"I heard they're going to hire people upstairs," the other replies.

Just then a message pops up on your screen: "Did you see that email? I checked our current numbers against last year's, and we're down as a whole."

Suddenly that carefree Monday morning drive feels a million miles away.

Everyone has heard a different story, and what doesn't help is the amount of confusing jargon the boss used. But the worst thing about this story is that it's not unusual. Communications lack clarity all the time.

We've all been the person confused by an email, and we've all sat through presentations that felt scattered. Maybe the speaker jumped from one idea to the next, sharing stories or anecdotes that did not quite connect. Maybe some of the stories were even interesting or funny. But in the end, we walked away unsure of what the core message was or what we were being asked to believe.

Buying a car is another common confusing practice, especially around the final price. Sometimes there's one upgrade that's thrown in "for free" while another one costs X dollars. But wait! There's a special running here. By the time we've gone through everything, the car seems to always end up being several thousand more than where we started, even with all the "free bonuses." While that may be common in the process, it often leaves the buyer feeling uneasy and slows down decision-making.

However, when your audience is clear about your message or when a listener is certain about your commitments or requests, they will trust your words and be more inclined to do what you ask them to do.

Clear as Mud

No one sets out to write a confusing speech, presentation, or email. But sometimes we think we need to pack in as much jargon as possible, create elaborate metaphors, or give the entire history of something in order to create the right context when really, we just need simplicity.

We need concise language. We need the shortest path from point A to point B and not the scenic route.

That's not to say we can never do those other things. There's a time and a place for long-winded stories, but a meeting isn't one of them. When you have a specific message or point to make, let clarity be your guide.

The audience's perception of your credibility and competence hinges on your ability to articulate your message clearly. A deep understanding of a topic allows for clearer explanations. A true expert can teach a subject simply and concisely.

In contrast, someone lacking true expertise might offer a complicated explanation filled with jargon and hesitations. Clarity assures the audience of your grasp of the subject matter, and it eliminates confusion and misunderstanding—two significant obstacles to trust.

When people feel overwhelmed, they become confused, and that confusion can quickly turn into fear, causing them to slip into a fight-or-flight response and either pull away or become passive and indecisive. For example, if an offer is too complex, it can create hesitation or even lead to a no. But when the message is simple and clear, it invites a direct response. A clear message appears more transparent and authentic, suggesting that you are not trying to conceal anything behind complicated language. A straightforward message calms the mind, enhances credibility, and increases trust.

Clarity fosters predictability and reduces perceived risk. A clear message reassures your audience by providing a sense of direction and allowing them to understand what to expect. It facilitates quicker, more effective decision-making.

Clarity also communicates both confidence and competence to the audience and yourself. When you have a clear understanding of your message, it shows the steady strength of your voice, the way your words rise and fall with intention, and how your eyes connect with your audience, drawing them in. Confidence also reveals itself in your body language, every gesture reinforcing what you say. Clarity shines through every aspect of communication.

Creating Clarity for Better Communication

Clarifying your message isn't difficult, but it does take some time and planning.

Prepare Concise, Structured Messages: True clarity often results in shorter presentations. The more concise and structured your message, the clearer it will be for your audience. The speaker who talks the longest on a topic isn't necessarily the most knowledgeable. In many cases, it simply means they haven't developed a deep enough understanding to explain it clearly and concisely.

When I'm working with top speakers, much of my time is spent helping them reduce the word count in their presentations. Fewer words make it easier for the audience to focus more intently on the key message.

A well-structured presentation typically includes the following:

- An opening sequence designed to connect with the audience and establish a clear purpose.

- A middle section that teaches content, normally divided into three or four digestible sections (typically the number of items people can remember easily, and fewer sections help keep the message simple).

- A clear ending with a focused call to action that asks the audience to take one specific next step rather than several.

This level of clarity will naturally shorten your presentations and significantly enhance your credibility.

Use Simple Language: One of the biggest challenges for experts is remembering the language they used before acquiring such in-depth knowledge. It's crucial to communicate using the language of your audience, not the specialized language of an expert.

If you're reading this book, chances are you're an expert in a particular field. I imagine you think about it constantly, read about it often, and bring it up in conversation without realizing it. When you spend that much time immersed in a subject, your vocabulary starts to shift. Because of this, I always make a conscious effort to simplify my language so the average consumer or customer can understand me easily.

Make it your goal to avoid jargon, unfamiliar acronyms your audience doesn't understand, industry-specific terms, and overly complex words and phrases. They can create a barrier between you and your audience. Clarity is best demonstrated through simple, jargon-free language.

Use Direct Language: If there's a sentence you're currently saying in twenty words, see if you can say it in ten. Speaking succinctly communicates clarity. Avoid fancy jargon, and say it in the simplest words possible. Don't add a lot of flowery language. Although big words and long, complex sentences can be considered good writing, they are rarely good speech. The more succinct and simple your language, the more clarity you will express.

Simplify your message to ensure immediate understanding. If you have to constantly explain and re-explain what you are talking about to the other person, you haven't explained it clearly enough. Make the message simple. Decide what your most important point is, and lead with that. Don't try to teach more than two or three things in one conversation. You have to pick your battles, and you should have a prioritized list of which battles are the most important.

Regularly Check Audience Understanding: Communication should always be a two-way street, whether you're addressing a large audience, having a one-on-one conversation, or speaking virtually. You need to consistently seek feedback.

During a live presentation, feedback can take many forms. You might notice subtle nods from listeners, hands raised in response to a question asked, quiet murmurs between neighbors, or audience members sharing their thoughts aloud.

In one-on-one conversations, feedback shows up differently. It might look like active listening, asking thoughtful follow-up questions, and taking a moment to consider your response before speaking. If you are doing 80 percent of the talking, you probably don't have clarity, and you certainly aren't sure if the other person understands you. Shoot for a 50/50 ratio between talking and listening. Put some thought ahead of time into the conversation and decide what questions you will ask to confirm the understanding of the person you are speaking to.

Being prepared in this way will go a long way to make sure the other person actually understands you. People who are willing to ask, "Does this make sense? Do you have any questions about this?" are confident in their message, and this level of confidence will create trust.

In virtual settings, you can use chat features, run online polls, or facilitate Q&A sessions to gauge audience comprehension.

These are proactive ways to ensure clarity in your message, which will help your audience better understand and significantly increase their trust.

Reinforce Your Key Messages Multiple Times: Great presentations have a central theme that connects the opening story to the closing remarks. Key messages within this theme should be revisited and reinforced throughout the presentation. Here's an easy formula to follow: Introduce your key message at the beginning as you outline what you'll cover, expand on it in each section of the teaching, and then summarize it clearly at the end. This repetition ensures that the audience hears your core message multiple times, reinforcing its clarity. Keep in mind that these same principles apply to one-on-one conversations, sales presentations, and all kinds of communication. There's no need to reinvent the wheel.

Create Contrasts: Whenever you are teaching a best practice or a new method, don't just explain the correct way; always contrast it with the incorrect or less effective way. Let's use morning routines as an example. Instead of simply sharing the best routine, tell a story about someone whose rushed morning led to a chaotic, unproductive day. Maybe they kept snoozing their alarm, which put them behind schedule. They skipped breakfast, and by midday, they were running on fumes.

Then contrast this with a story of someone who follows a structured morning routine. They get a full night's sleep, wake up on time, and never skip breakfast because they know they need energy to take on a full day. Their morning sets the tone, and it shows in their productivity. This contrast helps the audience clearly understand the value of your message.

Spatial Use of the Stage (and Visual Pivoting): Many speakers move around the stage. While some movement might be due to nerves, purposeful movement can enhance your message. My advice is to move with intention. One powerful way to use stage movement is to create contrasts, which, as mentioned earlier, clarifies your message.

Contrast helps people learn by showing them not just the right way but also the wrong way. To further emphasize this contrast, use the stage space strategically.

Try this: Start on one side of the stage (e.g., the right) when describing the incorrect way of doing something and the negative outcomes associated with it. Then, as you transition to explaining the correct way, move to the opposite side of the stage (e.g., the left). This creates two visual anchor points for the audience. Throughout the rest of the presentation, you can refer back to these "before" and "after" positions, even during your offer.

Let's say you're selling a new, environmentally friendly cleaning product. You might begin on one side of the stage, your "wrong way" side, describing how people have traditionally cleaned with harsh chemicals that leave residue and harm the environment. Then, as you introduce your new product, move to the other side, "the right way side," highlighting its residue-free, chemical-free, and eco-friendly properties. This spatial contrast reinforces your message. Interestingly, audience members often recall these stage positions when discussing the presentation later.

If you are presenting virtually, you can achieve a similar effect through a "left-right pivot." Even while seated, you can subtly shift your posture or use the left and right sides of your screen to represent the "before" and "after," creating a visual contrast for your online audience. This spatial or visual contrast powerfully demonstrates the clarity of your message, which in turn builds trust.

Use Visual Aids and Examples for Clarity: Many people are visual learners. Incorporating visual aids such as sales collateral or presentation slides can significantly enhance clarity. It's crucial that your visuals are perfectly aligned with your verbal message, using the same key themes and clear language. That means employing simple slides with concise visual messages that reinforce your spoken words rather than overwhelming slides packed with text.

For example, imagine you're giving a presentation on the benefits of financial planning. Your verbal message highlights three key areas: saving, investing, and budgeting. A strong visual would be a simple slide with a clean graphic showing those three categories side by side, each labeled clearly. That single image reinforces what you're saying without distracting or overloading the audience.

Now compare that to a slide filled with dense paragraphs explaining each concept. The audience ends up reading instead of listening, and the message gets lost. When your visuals are aligned with your verbal message, they work together to create clarity.

The clearer your message is, the fewer slides you'll need. If it takes a hundred slides to convey your point, your message likely lacks clarity. Simple, well-designed visuals help the audience grasp your message more effectively.

Visual Options Beyond Slides: Visuals are necessary for reinforcing the clarity of your message. While many think of PowerPoint or Keynote slides as the only option, you actually have three main types of visuals.

1. Prepared Slides: These are created in advance and presented in sequence. While useful, overuse can be detrimental. A presentation with an excessive number of slides (e.g., over a hundred in thirty minutes) might suggest a lack of clarity and can overwhelm the audience, hindering decision-making and eroding trust. Use fewer, simpler slides that directly support your message.

2. Live Visuals: These are created in real time during your presentation, such as using a flip chart or whiteboard. You might start with a blank page and develop bullet points or drawings as you speak. That can be engaging, but be mindful of spending too much time with your back to the audience. If your visuals vary significantly between presentations, creating them live might be more effective than preparing slides.

3. Three-Dimensional Visuals (Props): These are physical objects you hold up to illustrate your points. Props can significantly increase audience engagement and attention. However, avoid overusing them. Three or four well-chosen props in a thirty- to forty-minute presentation can be impactful.

Effective presentations combine these visual options: *some* prepared slides, *some* live visuals, and *a few* well-placed props. The key is to ensure that every visual is simple, directly aligned with your message, and used to reinforce it, not create confusion. Visuals are a powerful tool for enhancing the clarity of your message, and a clear message is directly linked to audience trust.

Lead with Your Key Points: Begin by leading with your key, most important points. Start the conversation by clearly stating your main objective or takeaway first. Don't save the best for last. Deliver the key information early, and acknowledge that it is a key point for your main objective. When we save our biggest objective or our key takeaway for the end of the conversation, it appears that we are hiding it or trying to have a big reveal moment. It can also appear that we aren't clear about what the most important thing is, that we're still deciding. This lack of clarity hurts confidence. This lack of confidence hurts trust.

Having clarity about what we're trying to communicate in a one-on-one conversation goes a long way in building trust with the other person in the conversation. So lead with your main objective, your key points, and your biggest takeaway. Don't save it for the end. Use the simplest, most succinct language you can possibly use to ensure immediate understanding. Regularly pause to confirm that the other person is understanding. Keep a good ratio of talking and listening during any conversation.

Creating Trust Activity

For this activity, pull out a copy of something you've written, like a presentation you gave recently or one you're working on. If you don't have a presentation, consider pulling out a few pages of anything else you're working on. Whatever it is, we're going to edit it for clarity.

First, let's look at the structure. Does your opening introduce the topic and lay out what you plan to discuss or teach the audience? Does the middle section walk the audience through that topic or that teaching in a logical manner anyone can easily follow? Does your ending contain a clear, one-step call to action? Before moving on, take time to reorganize accordingly. Put your strongest points first, insert spots to check on audience clarity, and don't worry about writing transitions yet. Just make sure you have the right pieces in the correct order.

Next, mark any areas where you use jargon, overly complicated language, or a long sentence or explanation for something simple. Play around with finding more concise ways to say the same thing or switching out layman's language for industry-specific terms.

Finally, review your slides against your revised speech. (Depending on what you pulled out, this may not apply.) Consider if you need to update the language or images to reinforce what you're saying or provide clarity for the audience.

When you've done what you can with it, set it aside for a few days and then read it with fresh eyes. At that point, I would also encourage you to compare the new and old versions to see how much stronger your presentation is with a little more clarity. After you've gone through this process a few times, infusing clarity into your writing and presentations becomes second nature and makes you a more trustworthy speaker.

CHAPTER 7

Trust Cue #5: Voice

Sometime last year, I found myself wandering around a new car lot near my house. I didn't need a new car at the time and hadn't really thought about buying one, but I wanted to check out a particular model that had just been released. This dealership had three or four of those new vehicles. As I peeked into the window of the car at the end, a salesperson walked over without my noticing.

"Hello?" he said in a soft voice, only a little louder than a whisper.

"Oh, hi," I replied, stepping back from the car, startled by his seemingly sudden appearance.

"Are you interested in this one?" he whispered again.

"Sorry, what did you say?"

"Do you want to know more about this car?" he asked. "It has a 335-horsepower engine and can go from zero to sixty in 5.5 seconds." His voice trailed off, his eyes wandering down to the info sheet on the clipboard in his hand.

As he started to lose his way, or so it seemed, another salesperson walked over and clapped him on the back.

"I see you're looking at our new models," the second salesperson said loudly and with authority, gesturing to the cars next to me. "I had a chance to test drive this one, and it is by far my favorite." Then he went on to tell me the same information the first salesperson began sharing but in a much more compelling and commanding tone. He spoke loudly enough that I could hear him over the noise of the traffic traveling the busy road next to the lot. He also paused from time to time and allowed me to visually inspect whatever he'd just mentioned.

The biggest difference between the two salespeople wasn't their knowledge or personal experience with the car in question; it was *how* they delivered that information.

Your voice is arguably your most powerful communication tool. It plays a significant role in determining whether or not your audience will listen to you and trust you. The truth is, *how* you say something often carries more weight than *what* you actually say. When you know how to use your voice, you create a stronger connection and trust with your audience.

Hearing Is Believing

Many people, even those who regularly speak in front of an audience, are unaware of how much their vocal delivery influences the way their audience perceives them. Ben Stein as the iconic teacher in the movie *Ferris Bueller's Day Off* is the perfect example of vocal delivery negatively affecting the audience. In the scene where he breaks down and explains the Smoot-Hawley Tariff Act of 1930, he speaks quickly, jumps from point to point, and doesn't allow time for the students to answer the questions he spits out, all while the kids have blank, slack faces. Not that the content isn't compelling, but the way Stein delivers the information in a deadpan voice at a fast speed nullifies any possible interest in it. He speaks as if he's there only for his own amusement and forgets to take the students on the ride with him. He also assumes that his words alone carry the message, overlooking how his voice can destroy his well-researched presentation. It's a great example illustrating that how you say something matters just as much as what you say.

Despite what we might think after hearing that scene or listening to the drone of "Bueller . . . Bueller . . . Bueller . . .," remember that your vocal pitch, speaking speed, and natural volume are not fixed traits. Singers and actors manipulate their voices all the time to create different characters or moods. Consider audiobooks—a single person often establishes a specific voice for every fiction character the listener encounters.

That takes a wide range of vocal qualities, including pitch and tone control, speed, and yes, volume. By becoming more aware of how your voice affects others, you can harness its power to build stronger connections and trust.

Moreover, when it comes to speaking in front of a group, your voice directly influences the perception of your trustworthiness and your audience's emotional comfort level with you. This emotional comfort is important because for an audience to take action, they need to feel secure enough to trust the validity, sincerity, and helpfulness of your offer. In any sales process, establishing that trust and emotional comfort is a key step, and your voice can significantly accelerate this process.

Your voice also creates lasting impressions and enhances recall. Using your voice effectively can make you memorable, ensuring that your message resonates with your audience long after you've spoken.

Oftentimes at the end of a speech or conversation, your goal is to get your listener(s) to act in some specific way. Don't think of that action as something that happens the moment your presentation ends. For many speakers, what they're really doing is planting a seed. That seed takes time to settle in, to be watered and nurtured before it finally begins to grow.

When the audience eventually needs what the speaker offers, their recollection of the message is often tied to the speaker's vocal delivery. A trustworthy and engaging voice leaves a more indelible mark.

Your Vocal Toolkit

While some aspects of your voice are innate, a significant portion can be shaped, improved, and developed over time. Whether you have a naturally deep or high pitch, a loud or quiet natural volume, or a tendency to speak quickly or slowly, you can learn to vary these elements. In fact, any time you present or even have a conversation with someone, there are four main qualities that influence your vocal performance: tone, pace, volume, and pauses. Mastering each of these will improve your ability to generate trust with your audience.

First, Become Aware of Your Voice: Before you can improve your vocal habits, you have to know what they are and acknowledge that while some aspects are innate, others are within your control. Believe it or not, many seasoned professionals have never given much thought to modifying their voice. But there is always value in maximizing your voice's effectiveness, especially by focusing on the changeable elements.

Modulate Tone (Pitch): The tone or pitch of your voice refers to how high or low you are speaking. While some individuals have naturally higher or lower voices due to the size of their vocal cords, a degree of control is possible. Just as singers train to expand their vocal range, speakers can also learn to modulate their pitch. If you have a naturally high voice, you might be able to lower it somewhat with practice. On the other hand, someone with a deep voice can learn to speak at a higher pitch when appropriate.

Awareness and conscious effort are key to expanding your vocal flexibility. There are several simple practices that can help improve your tone.

- Record yourself speaking, and then listen back and pay attention to the moments where your voice naturally rises and falls. Those are opportunities to add emotion and emphasis. If you're comfortable with it, you could also seek feedback from others or even have your vocal characteristics (tone, pace, volume, pauses) analyzed electronically to receive valuable insights.

- Read a passage aloud with intention, experimenting with different tones such as excitement, curiosity, or sincerity.

- Try vocal warm-ups like humming, lip trills, or sliding between low and high notes to help you gain better control of your pitch.

Control Your Pace (Speed): While everyone has a natural speaking pace or rhythm, influenced by habit and upbringing, you can consciously adjust your speaking speed with a little practice. When your voice stays calm and steady, it sends a message of reliability and predictability. It helps your audience feel like they can trust you and lowers risk. Conversely, rapid speech, abrupt shifts in volume, and erratic pauses can create an impression of unreliability and increased risk, regardless of the truth of your message.

To be an effective speaker, it also helps to adjust your pace to suit your content. When narrating a story, a consistently quicker (not erratic) pace can be engaging. However, when teaching important content or discussing emotionally significant points, slowing down your pace enhances comprehension and emotional connection. Matching your pace to your message creates consistency, which builds trust and conveys emotional warmth and sincerity.

If you struggle with pacing yourself, try practicing with a script and marking natural pauses or line breaks to guide your delivery. Reading a passage aloud at a slower, intentional pace can help you get comfortable with speaking more deliberately. Tools like metronomes or timers can keep you aware of your rhythm and prevent you from unintentionally speeding up. You can also implement breathing between each thought, which will allow you to keep yourself steady and consistent with your delivery.

Your pacing can also add warmth to your voice if you speak at a steady, slightly slower pace, and pause strategically throughout a conversation or presentation. Smiling genuinely, making eye contact, rounding out consonants (so they're not staccato and sharp), and leaning closer to the other person at appropriate times from an appropriate distance can also enhance the warmth of the conversation, and by extension, your voice.

Vary Your Volume: Many people consistently speak at either a high or low volume, never taking time to vary it or adjust based on, well, anything—setting, audience, or interest level. The most effective and trustworthy speakers modulate their volume, speaking quietly at certain times and more loudly at others to create emphasis, foster emotional comfort, and convey confidence, warmth, and trustworthiness. The first step is recognizing your current volume level, followed by learning to control it and understanding when to use different volume levels for maximum impact. A soft voice similar to a whisper is meant for quiet settings. A conversational volume is normally someone's natural speaking tone. A projected volume works best for speaking to a group in a larger room. Pay attention to how each one feels in your throat and body as you speak, and notice how it changes the tone and delivery of your message.

Take Time to Pause: Silence is as important as speech in verbal communication. A good balance of speaking and silence makes a speaker easy to listen to and influences their perceived trustworthiness, yet some speakers rarely pause, creating an exhausting experience for the listener.

Others use pauses that are excessively long, leading to audience confusion or concern. Great speakers understand the strategic use of pauses. They incorporate timed pauses to allow the audience to process information and create emotional resonance while avoiding doubt or confusion. Knowing the appropriate length of pauses, placing them strategically, and maintaining the right ratio of speaking to silence are crucial elements of effective communication.

Two key places for pauses are at emotional turning points in stories and after delivering a major point. Pausing after a significant statement gives your audience time to process and retain the information. Avoid immediately rushing past key points. A well-timed pause creates emphasis, encourages the audience to lean in and pay attention, and facilitates information retention, leading to a more lasting impression and better recall of your message.

One way to practice intentional pausing is to rehearse with a script, pausing briefly at *every comma*. This may seem excessive, but if you're not used to pausing, it will feel very uncomfortable at first. Exaggerating the pause in practice will help you get over the fear of silence during presenting, and eventually it will feel natural. You can also mark your script with slashes for short pauses and double slashes for longer ones throughout your presentation. If it still feels awkward to pause, find a speaker or communicator you admire and study how they use pauses. Imitate their rhythm until you develop your own.

Finally, Control Your Nerves: A nervous or unsteady voice can take away from your confidence and your audience's confidence in you. Nerves can manifest physically, including a shaky voice, often due to a lack of oxygen stemming from anxiety. Practicing deep breathing can stabilize your voice. Inhale deeply through your nose, allowing your belly to expand, and exhale slowly through your mouth. Repeating this several times before speaking can calm your nerves and result in a steadier, calmer, and more authoritative voice. If your voice begins to waver mid-speech, take a moment for a deep breath to regain composure. Maintaining a steady and calm tone fosters trust, reduces perceived risk, and projects confidence and authority.

The most effective communicators, whether on stage or in conversation, consciously manage these vocal qualities to cultivate emotional warmth and sincerity, project confidence and authority, build emotional comfort, and leave a lasting impression. How you say the words you speak is just as important as the specific words you are choosing. By slowing your pace, lowering your pitch, and adding warmth to your voice, you can convey confidence, steadiness, and trustworthiness. Hear the difference it can make for you.

Creating Trust Activity

I'm sure at this point you already know what I'm going to ask you to do. Record yourself as you give a presentation; then listen and rate the vocal qualities of your voice. Recording yourself giving the presentation or speech to an actual audience instead of only speaking to yourself in the mirror will give you the best experience of your vocal presentation. If you are unable to do that, do your best to put yourself as much in the mindset of a live presentation as possible. Why? Because we get nervous in front of others, and we may stumble at certain points or rush through others. You need to know where those spots are and what they sound like in order to correct them.

I would encourage you to listen to the recording a few times. First, simply close your eyes and hear your words. Then, listen while following along with a print-out of your speech, marking places where you could insert a pause, speed up or slow down, raise or lower your volume, change your tone, and so on. It may take a few listens to mark it to your liking.

Then practice, practice, practice.

When you feel good about your integrated changes, and if you're so inclined, record yourself again and listen back. You'll be amazed by how much of a difference your improved vocal presentation can make.

CHAPTER 8

Trust Cue #6: Empathy

When I started outlining the Trust Factors, I was only thinking about professional speakers or people giving presentations to large audiences. The first five Trust Factors have obvious applications in speaking to audiences. They establish your qualifications as an expert on a specific topic, help you organize your points in a logical way that thoughtfully leads the audience through whatever you're speaking about, and most importantly create trust between you and a roomful of strangers.

But something you may not consciously connect with when speaking to a group or a one-on-one sales meeting is empathy. It is one of the most powerful Trust Factors in this book.

The further I dove into each concept, it became clear that Trust Factors are essential to every conversation *and* every presentation, whether that happens between two people or two hundred people, from a stage, a doctor's office, a sales floor, or a classroom. When we strip trust down, at the heart of it all, we're trying to make genuine connections with others. That's where empathy comes in.

If you ask most people what fosters trust, the word *empathy* comes up most often. Empathy is about demonstrating genuine care and understanding for another person. When someone displays empathy, it can significantly deepen the emotional connection and rapport you have with your audience, enhancing mutual respect and trust.

Empathy encourages people to share more openly, which leads to better communication between individuals or groups. It also shows that you are sensitive to other people's needs. Whether you're addressing a large audience or engaging in a one-on-one conversation, showing empathy is key for any speaker.

Empathy Exists Everywhere

We've all seen or experienced someone with a lack of empathy, right? They're dismissive of others' thoughts and feelings, or self-focused. They think others are weak or too sensitive, don't consider other viewpoints valid, can't see past their own experience, and generally don't respond when other people are visibly hurting, among other things. It could be the teacher who says your question is stupid, the boss who waves away your ideas for the new product because they don't support them, or the salesperson who walks away from you mid-sentence when she learns you don't want to buy the car today.

But in the setting of a presentation to a large audience, what does it look like? It's the presenter who ignores the needs of the people in the seats, who doesn't clarify points or answer questions (or even consider questions valid), who presents a one-sided argument without addressing the other side (because it doesn't exist), and who can't understand what you don't understand (because it's obvious, right?). It's the person who fails to see the other people in the room. Because even if you're standing on the stage alone, you're never having a one-sided conversation.

Without empathy, you inevitably create distance between you and your audience. They can't trust you if you don't *see* them, if you don't acknowledge what they need from you, and if you don't take the time to build connections with them. They know if you only see them as dollar signs on a spreadsheet or if you don't think their questions are valid.

Indifference to the needs of your audience will kill your presentation. No matter where you are and what you're speaking about, you must always remember the experiences of *who* is in the audience.

Cultivating Empathy Everywhere, Even from the Stage

At the heart of empathy is understanding and feeling with another person, which is possible to do even from behind a podium or in a lab coat. While it's an internal state of being, there are plenty of ways to convey your understanding to the person or people in front of you, and in turn create real connections with your audience and build trust.

Begin with Active Listening: In a one-on-one or small group conversation, avoid dominating the conversation or solely focusing on getting your points across. Pay attention to the balance between your talking and listening. If you're speaking from a stage, you can employ this technique through audience engagement. Allow time for people to ask questions. As each person speaks, focus on what they're saying. As you begin to respond, acknowledge that you've heard them and understand what they're asking by affirming their situation using the rest of the tips in this section.

You will be able to tell when someone feels heard and engaged. They visibly relax because they feel safe in the conversation. They may also nod and use body language or physically lean into the conversation, even in a large conference room. However, if they push back against your assessment of their statement, then start over and find clarity through asking open-ended, thoughtful questions.

Validate and Reflect Others' Emotions Back to Them: Too many people go into a conversation or a presentation trying to convince the other person(s) of something. That mindset immediately indicates that you think your opinion is more important than theirs, which destroys trust. But through validation and reflection of the others' emotions and opinions, you demonstrate empathy and can build trust.

How can you acknowledge someone's feelings or point of view? After they speak, you briefly restate their feelings or the essence of their statement in your response to confirm that you heard and understood them correctly. You don't have to agree with those feelings to acknowledge that they're feeling them. You don't even have to relate to what they're feeling to acknowledge that the other person has them. They just need to feel heard and understood. It shows that you are actively listening and thoughtfully considering what the other person is saying. That builds trust.

For example, look at how people might respond to a setback. Some quit, and others try harder. If a frequent quitter expresses, "I want to quit right now," and you, as the person who tries harder, responds, "You shouldn't quit. You should try harder," you have just invalidated their feelings, and they will shut down. A better response would be, "I understand why you might want to quit right now, and I'm sure you're not the only person who has had that feeling in this situation."

This quickly and genuinely acknowledges and validates their feelings and demonstrates your empathy.

Taking it further, the most effective speakers understand the language, primary concerns, and overall emotion of their audience. They weave this understanding into their message, validating and reflecting the audience's perspective from the outset of their presentation. This is sometimes called "pacing." Taking it a step further, "leading" involves first validating the audience's current emotional state and then guiding them toward a new understanding or perspective.

Imagine you're speaking to someone who's having difficulties with a transition or new beginning or ending in their personal life. If you say, "You should be excited at the new possibilities," you'll most likely cause them to put their guard up because you didn't acknowledge what they were actually feeling, which could be stress, anxiety, frustration, and so on. But if you begin with, "I know the last few months have felt uncertain and heavy for you," you're pacing by joining them emotionally. Then follow up with, "And even in the midst of that, I believe there's a beautiful path forward for you." Now you're leading. You've validated their reality first and then pointed them toward something better.

Ask Open-Ended Questions to Understand Perspectives: In many conversations, especially sales interactions, questions are often used to identify weaknesses for persuasive purposes. However, when asking questions, your primary goal is to genuinely understand the other person's perspective, not just find an opportunity to sell. Open-ended questions, which encourage detailed responses rather than simple yes or no answers, are far more effective in uncovering someone's true viewpoint.

For example, if you're a consultant assessing a company's team dynamic, instead of asking, "Would you say your team is underperforming?" you might ask, "How are things going with your team lately?" That small shift invites a fuller answer and creates space for real insight. From there, you can explore further with questions like, "What do you think is causing that?" or "What have you already tried to improve?" When questions are rooted in curiosity, conversations become more honest.

In addition, open-ended questions demonstrate our curiosity about the other person and, in turn, our empathy for them. When we are truly interested in learning and helping someone, not just persuading or selling to them, we can accelerate the trust process by going deeper than the shallow conversation level. That encourages the sharing of deeper emotions and deeper thoughts, which forges relationships and trust. Remember, this is all about seeing the individual humans in your audience, not numbers or dollar signs.

Many times, a conversation will start at a shallow level: *How is your day today? My day was good.* But you can accelerate the trust process with deeper, more thoughtful questions: *What makes your best days your best days? What was it about that incident you just told me about that made it so meaningful for you?* This communicates that you are interested in a long-term relationship, not a transactional relationship, and will help in the trust-building process.

Practice Patience and Avoid Interrupting: Resisting the urge to interrupt someone in the middle of their response is a challenging but essential skill for building empathy. This is particularly true when you disagree or possess information the other person lacks. Those who speak professionally are often eager to share their knowledge, and that enthusiasm can sometimes lead to interruptions. Similarly, a statement might trigger a thought you want to express, leading to an unintentional interruption. Patiently listening and consciously avoiding interruptions is a key discipline in developing empathy.

Respond Thoughtfully and Sensitively to Concerns: It's common to walk into a conversation or presentation with a mental checklist of things we want to say. But when we're too focused on our own points, we can miss what's actually happening around us. When we are solely concerned with delivering our message, we can become "tone deaf" to what preceded our speaking or what follows. Being mindful of what the person you are speaking to has just said and responding appropriately, thoughtfully, and sensitively to their concerns are vital for effective communication and building trust.

When addressing an audience, pay attention to group dynamics, acknowledge the previous speaker's message, and be aware of any relevant situations in the room. Recognizing the hosts of the event and acknowledging the audience for their efforts and current circumstances also build trust quickly. Great speakers often begin by acknowledging the speaker before them, reinforcing their message to show understanding of the context.

They also recognize the hosts and the audience for their contributions and current situations. If there are any relevant industry trends, current events, or specific challenges the audience is facing (e.g., economic downturn, sensitive topics), acknowledge them early in the presentation, thus fostering trust between the speaker and the audience.

Empathy can go a long way in accelerating the trust-building process. In my company's surveys of people about what caused them to have trust in another person, empathy is one of the most commonly expressed indicators of trust. Use reflective listening to restate what the other person has said in the conversation and to confirm your understanding. Express curiosity with thoughtful questions that encourage deeper sharing, and validate the feelings of the other person, whether or not you agree or relate. Empathy will lead to demonstrating that you care and are respectfully listening to the other person. That, in turn, will build trust.

Creating Trust Activity

This may already be part of how you naturally interact with others, but for your empathy exercise, I want you to focus on three things: active listening, validating, and asking open-ended questions. These are the three foundational pieces to enhance empathy. If you can practice them so they become a natural part of your interactions, the rest will flow.

For just one day, use these three skills in *every interaction*, no matter how long or short the conversation. That might sound like it will take a lot of work, but when people can feel your empathy, they will open up. They will respond more positively. They will look forward to seeing you. And they will usually respond with empathy of their own.

As you move throughout your day, reflect on how flexing your empathy muscle changes your interactions. Did your relationship grow deeper? Did the interaction feel more substantial? Do you feel more seen and heard?

If you already practice active listening, validate others, and ask open-ended questions, reflect on your last presentation or speech. Do you do those things from the stage? Are there places where you can enhance your empathy or pause for a moment to connect with the audience? Take time to note opportunities for empathy and trust-building, and begin to build them into your audience interactions. You'll be amazed by how enriched your audience interactions will become.

CHAPTER 9

Trust Cue #7: Commonalities

Raise your hand if you've ever had this conversation when meeting someone for the first time:

"It's nice to meet you," you start. "Where are you from?"

"Here," they respond.

"It's a nice town. Do you like it?"

"No."

"What do you do?"

"I work in an office."

"Do you like what you do?"

"No."

"Did you see the [insert sporting event] on Saturday? Nail-biter."

"No."

"Have you seen [insert name of new movie]? I saw it last week, and it was so good."

"No."

"Tried a new restaurant? I'm always looking for recommendations."

"No."

By this point, you're probably thinking of ways to just walk away without being awkward.

"Oh, there's Martin. I need to go say hi, but it was interesting to meet you." (This avoids the lie that it was great to meet them while still being a little nice.) And you walk away. End scene.

Try this revision:

"It's nice to meet you," you start. "Where are you from?"

"Here," they respond.

"It's a nice town. Do you like it?"

"Yes, I grew up here, but I was actually born in [insert your hometown]. I still have a lot of family there, so I visit often."

"That's where I'm from! I went to [insert name of local restaurant] last night, and it reminded me of [insert name of hometown restaurant]."

"Oh my gosh. I never thought about it, but you're right! I love the . . ." and then the conversation is up and running.

Which one do you prefer? Which one feels better? Which one will you remember?

Unless you're Oscar the Grouch, it's instinctual to look for commonalities with a new person. The first thing we usually do when meeting someone is ask them about themselves. "Where are you from?" Do you have children?" or "What do you do for a living?" We're trying to learn who they are, what their experience has been, and if we share any of that. But have you stopped to think about why we ask these questions? Why do we try to find commonalities with complete strangers?

We're trying to see if we align with them, if we understand and share their experiences, and, at a deeper level, if we're safe with them, in this together, and yes, if we can trust them. Commonalities enhance comfort, rapport, and familiarity. They establish a record of shared past experiences and authenticity. They can improve our credibility and even help us empathize. They create bonds that extend beyond the boundaries of a given situation. They make small talk at the coffee station in the office less awkward. And they can form the foundation of a bigger, stronger relationship, which is what this is all about.

When There Are No Bonds That Bind Us

When we don't have anything in common with the person next to us, the chasm of differences between us can seem impossible to cross. Our minds immediately create an "us" and "them" situation. We don't know what to talk about, and we may not know how to explain something in a way they'll understand. We may be less inclined to cooperate with them or ask for help from them. And we may be more inclined to disagree and withhold understanding. It can be harder to bond and definitely harder to trust.

Overcoming this lack of commonalities isn't impossible. But it is significantly hard. Your credentials and expertise, past experiences, and authenticity have to do a lot of heavy lifting to fill in the gaps. However, if your goal is building trust, it's worth the work to find common ground, any common ground, and build on it.

Discovering Common Ground

Like building empathy, one of the most important things you can do to build trust is to seek out common ground, but that's not always easy to do, whether one-on-one or from the stage. But with a little planning, in-the-moment flexibility, and persistence, you can usually establish enough commonalities to build trust with your audience.

Identify Common Ground and Highlight Shared Experiences Early in Your Interactions: Before you write your speech or presentation or before you meet with a new client, take time to learn about them (if possible) or reflect on what their experiences may have been. If you used to work in a similar field or environment, consider how you felt or what you thought about it in relation to what your audience might be going through—in other words, try practicing empathy before you've met. Consider how you might highlight that common experience or those feelings early in your presentation. In the case of a new client, check out their business profile to see if you have similar backgrounds, or early in your conversation, ask about their schooling or where they grew up—finding what you have in common

When creating your presentation or meeting that person for the first time, focus on identifying these shared experiences near the beginning. Then as your interaction unfolds, look for things that you and the other person(s) have both done. For example, if a question asked in the middle of your presentation or conversation unlocks a commonality, take a moment to highlight that fact. That may require you to be flexible or spontaneous, but it will help your rapport with the audience.

If direct shared experiences are lacking, seek out similar experiences and emphasize them. Dedicate more time to highlighting those commonalities rather than your unique experiences, at least in this early stage. Additionally, highlight shared backgrounds. Where you are from, similar upbringings, and other commonalities can quickly build trust in initial interactions.

Explicitly Note Shared Values or Goals: In your research, you may have found commonly shared values with the individual or the company. Reference these commonalities relevant to the context of the conversation early in the conversation or presentation. If you share faith with someone you're talking to or if you agree that integrity is an important part of the way you operate, mention it. If you believe in teamwork, value family, or value a work-life balance, reveal that information. Aligning the conversation around those shared values will accelerate the trust-building process.

If you can't find a natural way to add your common values or goals to your presentation or discussion, try telling a personal story that highlights those points. That not only highlights your common value or goal but also builds your past experiences and related credibility and authenticity. Ensure that the stories you tell reveal values and aspirations that resonate with your audience rather than those that might create a sense of difference. Those initial stages are for connection, not instruction.

Leverage Mutual Connections or Networks: One of the most potent commonalities to leverage is mutual acquaintances. Try to find someone you and the other person have in common and mention that connection. In the case of an organization, maybe you can share a story about how you know the founder or someone people in the audience might know and/or admire. That shared connection can significantly accelerate trust through third-party validation and the assumption of similarity. If your friend likes and trusts someone, you're more likely to like and trust them too because your friend has already vetted them.

If a mutual acquaintance isn't apparent, try to find a shared group membership. Shared group affiliations can also create common ground. Perhaps you were both involved in scouting, or you belong to the same professional organization. Group affiliations often reflect shared values, goals, and identity. Major sporting events also create shared experiences and memories that can be used to build trust in interactions. Even being users of the same software or app can contribute to building trust.

While the prevalence of weather discussions often stems from the fact that it's a universal commonality, I'd steer clear here. It highlights the fact that you literally have nothing else in common other than the sun above.

Adapt Language and References to Resonate with Specific Audiences: One of the most important skills for any speaker or salesperson is to describe the problem you address in the language of the consumer, not the expert. Adjusting your language and the references in your examples to align with those of your listener(s) is a crucial aspect of building trust. It taps into empathy through reflecting the fact that you understand the issues the listener is having and that you know how to remedy the situation because you've been there.

Oftentimes, a speaker has a much deeper understanding of their topic and its solutions than their audience, and that's why you're there. However, that can lead to the use of unfamiliar and inaccessible language. The same applies in sales conversations. Salespeople, immersed in their product or service, can inadvertently use jargon that is foreign to a first-time inquirer. They might make logical leaps that their audience can't follow. Slowing down your presentation and adapting your language to match that of your prospect is essential for building trust quickly. When the person you are talking to articulates the problem using the exact language you were thinking, trust increases. When their frustrations mirror your own in their expression, trust deepens.

"Us" Not "I": When you frame the conversation around *me* and *I* versus *you*, you create a separate experience from your audience rather than uniting with them. Our whole purpose in this chapter is to connect with the other person(s). So from the beginning of your presentation or conversation, focus on using "us" language rather than "I" language. Frequently include words like *us* or *we* to subtly reinforce this commonality and connection.

In general, using any of the seven Trust Factors from Chapters 3 through 9 in isolation will increase the trust during a conversation or presentation. But when you combine them and integrate the strategies into your daily interactions, speeches, and presentations, you will master your ability to build trust quickly. Utilize past experiences, build credibility, share weaknesses to build authenticity, speak succinctly to build clarity, use your voice to express empathy, and always mention shared experiences and commonalities to build trust and achieve the results you want.

Creating Trust Activity

Every time you create a presentation or are hired to give a speech, take time to reflect on who is in the audience. If this is a business, what does the business do? What do these people care about? What might you, they, and the topic all have in common? Using your reflection, take time to revise your talk, adding in moments to connect through commonalities. Look for opportunities to shift your language from "I" or "me" statements to "we" and "us" statements. Find ways to group yourself with your audience and employ empathy when discussing the problem or obstacle to begin combining the seven Trust Factors and unlocking their trust-building potential that much faster.

I know it might sound like common sense, but trust me, it's not. But if you can create that connection, you're building trust and improving your chances of booking that same event in the future.

CHAPTER 10

Taking to the Stage

As you've seen throughout this book, the seven Trust Cues apply to building relationships in any setting—one-on-one or between presenter and audience. But speakers have an additional aspect to consider: their stage presence. As we talked about in Chapter 4 (Credibility), how you present can build or break a listener's confidence in your abilities. In this chapter, we'll illustrate how your ability to command a stage can engage or bore your audience.

Some of this information will seem familiar by now, but here we're specifically addressing how to use the Trust Cues to put together a great presentation. Whether at a conference, workshop, theater, or simple work presentation, there are three fundamental aspects to consider when speaking to any group: the words you choose, how you deliver those words, and your physical movement as you speak.

- The words you select are undoubtedly important. You want to articulate your message in a way that builds trust with your audience. Omitting crucial information or adding unnecessary details can erode the trust they have in you.

- Equally important is your delivery—how you say those words. You might have the perfect message, but if your tone of voice is off, or if your speaking pace is too rapid or too slow, it can negatively impact the audience's trust in you.

- Finally, your physical presence and movement as you speak can either enhance or detract from the audience's trust. Whether it's the movement of your hands or your overall presence on stage, how should you move to maximize the audience's trust?

Mastering these details, along with the seven Trust Cues, will help you build trust in any setting and improve your conversion rate practically overnight.

What You Say and the Order to Say It

When you stand before an audience, the words you choose carry significant weight in establishing trust, and we've noted the key elements to intentionally incorporate when fostering this crucial connection—common past experiences, authenticity, and empathy. But you may be wondering about the most effective way to include them in your presentation.

In the case of common experiences, the most impactful presentations often begin with a personal story, and the most resonant personal stories are those that connect with the audience on a relatable level. When selecting your opening story, ask yourself: *What story can I tell that will prompt the maximum number of people in the room to nod in recognition and think, "That same thing happened to me"?* That is your most powerful opening.

Many speakers err by starting with a story that highlights their differences from the audience rather than their similarities. While there is certainly a place for sharing unique experiences later in your presentation, especially if you possess exceptional expertise or a distinctive process, the beginning should focus on shared ground.

After establishing a connection with your opening story, it's crucial to make a road map of the rest of your presentation. Clarity breeds confidence, and one of the best ways to showcase clarity is with this road map. It simply means providing a clear preview of what you will teach. By outlining your key points at the beginning, you demonstrate clarity and that your presentation is a well-structured message, not a random collection of anecdotes or facts.

The most effective speakers also include a time element in their road map: "In the next thirty minutes, I'm going to teach you these three things." Then, precisely thirty minutes later, the speaker reminds the audience of the two promises they made and kept: the time commitment and the content delivery. A statement like "Just thirty minutes ago, I said I would teach you these three things; now let's review what we've covered," effectively highlights your reliability in fulfilling promises, a significant driver of trust based on past experiences.

Once you've established the road map, you'll want to move into the teaching portion of your presentation. Here you'll address the problem your audience faces. Be sure to convey empathy for your listener's current situation here. Using the language of your audience to describe the problem they face demonstrates that you understand their perspective and can see the world through their experiences.

Intentionally weave in stories and examples of areas where you are not proficient and mistakes you have made. This openness about your weaknesses helps the audience see you as genuine and relatable, significantly contributing to trust. It also establishes your credibility—you've been there, done that, and can help them with the same.

Throughout the presentation, remain mindful of the context and express empathy for the audience using their own language. Reference the immediate context, the speaker before you, the event itself, industry trends, or global economic conditions. That shows you are aware of and care about their reality and respect their challenges. Expressing empathy through your words helps the audience develop greater trust in you.

Furthermore, be sure to incorporate examples, stories, and case studies that illustrate how you have successfully solved problems for others. Because credibility is so closely linked to trust, sharing narratives that demonstrate your ability to deliver solutions for issues similar to those your audience faces is essential. These examples, often taking the form of case studies or personal stories of helping others, provide concrete evidence of your expertise.

Next is the call to action—what do you want your audience to do? When you make these calls to action, ensure you have woven in stories that establish your credibility in solving the listeners' problem, your track record of fulfilling promises, your clear understanding of their needs, and your empathy for their struggles.

Then, at the conclusion, summarize what you have taught, reinforcing that you have delivered on your initial promise.

By strategically incorporating these elements into your presentation, you will build trust with your audience more quickly and more effectively.

How You Say It

Once you have clarity on the points you want to make and the order in which to make them, consider how you will deliver those words. As we discussed in Chapter 7, the way you use your voice on stage can significantly impact the level of trust your audience has in you as a speaker.

By now, you've been working on the four main aspects of your voice. Here's how to take each of those to the next level and take control of the variables to optimize your presentation.

The first variable is the pace of your speaking. Speaking too quickly can make you appear inauthentic, not transparent, and lacking confidence. Conversely, speaking too slowly can lead the audience to perceive you as unclear and unsure of your message. The good news is that there is an optimal speaking speed for each part of a speech, and achieving the right pace can increase audience trust. You'll also notice that as you move between these parts and speeds, your pace will vary. That's natural and what you want.

When telling a story, you can generally increase your pace as the audience is focused on the narrative flow rather than specific details or notetaking. However, when you reach the emotional climax of your story, slow your pace to allow the audience time to emotionally connect and react.

When teaching content, a slower pace is crucial as the audience needs time to process the information and may be taking notes. Slow down even further when delivering your most important points. Great speakers don't typically raise their volume, pound the podium, or point to emphasize key messages; instead, they elongate their words and slow their speaking pace, naturally drawing attention to what's most important.

When you transition to your call to action or offer, many speakers instinctively speed up due to nervousness. Consciously monitor your pace during this section, maintaining a steady, medium-slow speed. Slow down on the most crucial aspects of your offer to avoid conveying a lack of transparency or confidence.

The next variable is your volume. Speaking too loudly or too quietly consistently is not ideal for building maximum trust. Vary your speaking volume. Speakers who maintain a high volume throughout their talk can cause audience fatigue, leading them to tune out. Conversely, a consistently low volume can project a lack of confidence and cause the audience to miss important words. A significant portion of any audience may have some degree of hearing loss, making a consistently quiet delivery problematic. That can lead the audience to miss trust-building elements in your talk.

The best approach is to modulate your volume. Speak at a medium volume most of the time, and at exciting points in a story or during certain content, increase your volume to create variation. When you reach the emotional climax of your story or your most important teaching points, lower your volume.

While it might seem counterintuitive, lowering your volume at these key moments will cause the audience to lean in and listen more intently. Varying your volume is a crucial technique for maintaining audience engagement. Comments like "That speaker yelled the whole time" or "That speaker was hard to hear" are indicators of ineffective volume control. Utilize measurement tools to assess the volume and variability of your voice while speaking. Having a range of volumes and consistently varying them projects confidence and increases trust.

The third variable to focus on is the tone or pitch of your voice. Some speakers have a naturally high pitch, while others have a deep, low voice. There is an optimal pitch range that tends to maximize audience trust, and that range can differ slightly between male and female speakers. Generally, most speakers can benefit from lowering their tone or pitch to build more trust. There's a reason why many successful female politicians on a national level often have deeper voices. While it's less common, it's also possible for your pitch to be too low.

Varying your pitch throughout your presentation is essential to avoid sounding monotone (remember Ben Stein), which can make you difficult to listen to, hard to focus on, and challenging to remember. By varying your pitch and predominantly delivering your message within the optimal trust range, you can project confidence and enhance audience trust.

The final variable we'll examine in how you say your words is pauses. Some speakers have virtually no pauses in their speech, creating a continuous stream of words that can be overwhelming and difficult to process. This lack of pausing makes it hard for the audience to learn, connect emotionally, or fully absorb the content, thus hindering trust. Conversely, excessively long pauses can make the audience wonder if you're okay or have forgotten your speech, projecting a lack of confidence and clarity that damages trust.

There is an optimal pause ratio for every speaker. Too few pauses prevent connection and trust; too many create doubt. The right number of pauses allows the audience to connect with you, learn from you, and trust you.

Many speakers have never consciously considered managing or even measuring these aspects of their delivery. We've all heard speakers we found boring, too fast, or monotone, but few of us have taken the step to measure these simple variables to ensure we are doing everything possible to build trust with our audience.

If you're having trouble with any of the voice variables, know that there are tools out there to measure the variation in your pitch, pace, tone, volume, or any other aspect of your voice. One that I helped develop and use with my coaching clients is TheVoiceAnalyzer.com. Measurement tools are more reliable and precise than audience opinions for determining if your voice is monotone, too fast, slow, high, low, loud, soft, and so on. What we measure we can improve, and what you improve will help us gain audience trust.

How to Move on Stage

How you move when you're on stage in front of an audience can significantly influence the level of trust you cultivate during your presentation. Speakers who move with purpose, with a clear reason behind their movement, and execute it confidently, project clarity and confidence, leading to increased trust. Conversely, random or constant movement, or a complete lack of movement, can signal a lack of confidence and cause trust to decline. Employing specific on-stage movement strategies can project confidence, enhance clarity, and ultimately increase audience trust.

Move with Purpose: There are three primary reasons to move on stage.

To Create Contrast: When teaching, it's often more effective to first illustrate the incorrect way to do something before presenting the correct approach, creating a clear contrast. This contrast aids memory retention and provides clarity, which in turn builds trust.

For example, when teaching about morning routines, first describe someone with a chaotic, unproductive morning, and then move to the other side of the stage to describe someone with a structured, successful routine. This visual contrast creates visual anchor points, helping the audience remember the correct method. Throughout your presentation, you can refer back to these stage positions to reinforce your teaching.

Audience members, especially visual learners, will often recall these positions even months later. If presenting online, you can achieve a similar contrast by pivoting at your hips within your video frame, using the left and right sides to represent the "before" and "after."

To Show the Passage of Time: When narrating a story that spans different periods, use your stage position to visually represent the timeline. For instance, begin on one side for childhood events, move to the center for young adulthood, and end on the other side for recent events. While it might seem counterintuitive (as time typically progresses left to right visually), for the audience, this left-to-right movement on stage creates a logical and easy-to-follow timeline, aiding comprehension and recall. Move confidently between these positions to build trust.

To Separate Your Topics: For presentations with multiple key teaching points, use different areas of the stage for each point. Present the first point on one side, the second in the center, and the third on the other side. This visual benchmarking of your presentation into a beginning, middle, and end enhances clarity and helps you present with more confidence. The audience gains a clear understanding of your structure and where you are in your presentation, increasing trust.

Avoid the following movement mistakes.

Moving Constantly or Randomly: Some speakers exhibit incessant movement, pacing back and forth or fidgeting with stage furniture. This conveys a lack of confidence and clarity—a lack of confidence because you never appear grounded and a lack of clarity because your movement seems aimless. This randomness diminishes audience trust.

Never Moving: Remaining static in one spot throughout your presentation can also project a lack of confidence, perhaps indicating fear of the audience, reliance on notes, or fear of forgetting your material. This lack of dynamism can decrease trust.

Master Your Stance

How you stand on stage also communicates clarity and confidence.

Closed Stance (hands clasped, arms crossed): This can suggest you are hiding or afraid, decreasing trust due to a perceived lack of confidence, transparency, or authenticity.

Open Stance (arms at sides, palms up): This projects authenticity and transparency, fostering confidence and increasing trust. Transitioning to an open stance, especially during your call to action, with arms pulled back and palms up, signals confidence in your offer and can improve conversion rates as well as trust.

Uneven Weight Distribution (leaning heavily on one leg): This often leads to a hyperextended and wobbling knee, which conveys nervousness and a lack of confidence. Shifting weight back and forth creates a distracting rocking motion. Instead, balance your weight evenly between your feet, positioned shoulder-width apart, and lean slightly forward onto the balls of your feet for greater stability. While movement is purposeful, be sure to maintain stillness during key moments.

Strategic Stillness: Avoid moving during the most crucial parts of your talk—when teaching your biggest points, during emotional turning points or climaxes in your stories, and when making your offer or call to action. Plant your feet center stage and remain still during those moments to emphasize their importance and project confidence and clarity, which builds trust.

Movement During Your Offer: Be particularly mindful of your movement during your call to action. Avoid breaking eye contact, adopting a closed stance, or moving backward on the stage, as these actions can signal a lack of confidence and transparency in your offer, hurting trust and conversion rates. Instead, maintain eye contact, an open stance with palms up, and either remain still or move slightly forward toward the audience to convey transparency and confidence.

Vertical Stage Positions: Consider utilizing the vertical space of the stage (near the audience, middle, far from the audience) strategically.

- **Far Position:** Best for teaching content
- **Middle Position:** Ideal for storytelling
- **Near Position:** Most effective for offers, calls to action, and emotional climaxes

Being in the appropriate vertical position for the type of speech you are delivering demonstrates a level of clarity that most speakers lack. Combining this with purposeful stillness during important moments in the correct position (far, middle, or near) projects confidence. This strategic use of stage space and movement will enhance both your conversion rate and your audience's trust.

Gaining the trust of your audience involves more than just the words you say and how you say them; it also encompasses how you move on stage. The more comfortable you are with how you command the stage and guide the audience through your presentation, the more confident you will be. And confidence only enhances your ability to build trust with your audience.

CHAPTER 11

Better Impact, Better Results

I've been in the speaking business now for many years. Throughout that time, I've had the chance to work with naturally gifted presenters and those just starting out. But no matter who I'm working with, this lesson arises almost every time: It takes more than a good script to make a good presentation, give a good speech, and most importantly, build trust with your listener.

I wrote this book to help professional speakers and people in relationship businesses learn how to build trust quickly and effectively. But on another level, I wrote this for my younger self, that newly graduated math teacher who didn't yet know how to connect with his students. Building trust is essential to establishing any kind of relationship, and yet trust can be hard to come by. Since COVID, doctors are not as trusted.

Jokes about crooked attorneys or used cars salespeople are still prevalent. And every day, we find more and more reasons to not trust. That's what makes the seven Trust Cues more important than ever.

If you're not getting the conversions you expect, if you're not connecting well with clients or audiences, if you're having trouble creating trust between you and your listener, practice the exercises in this book. If you want to take it to the next level, use a tool like the Voice Analyzer to receive clear, hard data about how to improve and what to improve to build trust faster.

The Trust Cues and the Voice Analyzer aren't just for an individual presenter or professional though. When all the employees for a business can build trust effectively, the business's sales increase exponentially. How do I know? That's what my clients are saying.

A business owner in the finance industry called and asked me about speaker coaching services and the Voice Analyzer specifically related to building trust. I asked him how he'd heard about my coaching, and it turned out that three of his employees had used the service.

"How many speakers do you want to train?" I asked him. "A few more?"

"No," he said. "I want all forty of our employees to go through the coaching and voice analysis."

"All forty?" I wasn't sure I'd heard him correctly.

"Yes, because we don't know who's going to greet someone at the front desk or answer the phone. We want everyone in our company to have the skills to build trust and establish relationships quickly."

Since this conversation, I've spoken with countless other business owners who understand the importance of trust and who have engaged our coaching services and Voice Analyzer for an entire staff. On average, we find that after analysis, we can improve any speaker's conversion rate with as few as three coaching sessions. How? Because the Trust Cues aren't just my opinion about what makes someone a better relationship builder. There's more than thirty years of research backing each Trust Cue. If you're interested in further reading, I've included a list of Additional Resources in Appendix B.

It all comes down to this: When we don't build trust effectively, we leave at least some of our impact on the table. With tools like this book and the Voice Analyzer, we can identify clear areas for improving our Trust Cues, which will result in higher conversion rates, better audience engagement, and business growth at unimaginable rates. But more than that, when we actively use the Trust Cues in our conversations and presentations, we build relationships with our listeners that outlast the meeting or speech. We leave a lasting impression, and most importantly, we create human-to-human connections.

Trust Cue Quick Review

Trust Cue #1: Past Experiences

Past experiences, whether told through story or demonstrated through in-person interactions, quickly establish our moral character and trustworthiness. They illustrate that we are dependable and follow through on our commitments and promises, as well as reinforce our future trustworthiness.

Prove your past experiences by:

- **Making small promises early—and always following through on them**
    - o Things like holding to meeting times, giving concrete steps for the audience to follow, and so on

- **Communicating your commitments and their fulfillment**

  o In a presentation, outline what you'll cover, and then review at the end how you indeed covered all the topics noted.

- **Checking in to confirm satisfaction**

  o Ask the audience if their questions have been answered or if your client is satisfied with whatever service or product you provided.

- **Addressing misunderstandings promptly**

  o When miscommunications arise—and they will—listen with empathy and respond without defensiveness. Explain your understanding of the situation, acknowledge any shortcomings, and work together to find a satisfactory resolution for all.

- **Owning your mistakes and implementing necessary changes**

  o Don't waste time giving excuses; acknowledge what happened and highlight how you have changed or plan to remedy the situation.

Trust Cue #2: Credibility

Credibility is whether or not your listener believes you are a reliable and knowledgeable source of information. How you present yourself, what you present, and your reputation (i.e., your past experiences) all affect your credibility.

Establish your credibility through:

- **Earning and communicating your relevant qualifications**

  o   Hang your diplomas and certificates, include your credentials in your signatures or on your presentation, and so on.

- **Providing evidence of your past successes**

  o   Like sharing your past experiences, include testimonials or stories of how you have helped others or satisfied customers or employers.

- **Choosing your timing**

  o   Trust levels are generally higher during the teaching portion of a presentation, so use that opportunity to share about your successes. If you wait until you've reached the call to action, it will come across as a sales tactic rather than a credibility-builder.

- **Leveraging endorsements from reputable sources and/or referencing a common third party**

  o   Include testimonials from well-known clients or clients with impressive titles. If possible, note names that would most likely be familiar to your audience.

- **Demonstrating continuous learning and improvement**

  o In the same way you would include past successes, talk about how you stay informed about industry standards and trends or current certifications you sought.

- **Providing immediate value**

  o Offer a few practical insights and concrete actionable steps the audience can take to improve their lives or address the topic at hand in their own lives.

Trust Cue #3: Authenticity

Authenticity lets your listener know you are grounded, transparent in your intentions and actions, and relatable. Trust is built when people act predictably and in ways that support their stated values.

Demonstrate your authenticity by:

- **Telling your story in a logical and coherent way—make sure it passes the "smell test"**

  o If something is illogical or doesn't quite add up, like "I gave up sugar and now I'm a millionaire," it gives the listener pause and throws your credibility and thereby your authenticity into question.

- **Regularly reflecting on your actions and beliefs**

  o On a personal note, check in with yourself to ask if your actions align with your beliefs.

  o In a speech or presentation, include small references to your faith or beliefs, "We did this on our way home from church one day . . ."

- **Communicating openly**

  o Be an active listener—hear what the other person is saying and thoughtfully consider your response before speaking.

- **Admitting your mistakes**

  o Like addressing your past misunderstandings, don't cover up your mistakes or the shortcomings of something. If they're relevant, state the facts of what happened or the facts of the shortcomings, and the listener will connect with your genuineness.

  o When you *only* note the highlights or best features, whatever you're saying won't pass the "smell test."

- **Aligning your words and actions—consistency is key**

  o Make sure your actions are aligned with your stated beliefs.

    ▪ Don't sell the wrong product to someone just to make a big sale—and let your listener know about this integrity.

- o Ensure that your body language and tone match the message you're sharing.

  - ▪ If you're talking about something sad or heavy, don't smile and speak with energy— lower your volume, slow your pace, and give the moment the reverence it deserves.

- **Seeking feedback**

  - o This is as simple as asking about your client's experience and if there is anything you can do to improve it.

- **Being present**

  - o Shut out distractions so you can focus on and engage with the speaker.

- **Expressing your honest intentions**

  - o When you clearly state your purpose for a conversation, you immediately demonstrate your transparency and sincerity, and in turn build with your listener.

Trust Cue #4: Clarity

Clarity infuses your words with certainty and by extension, trust. When your listener can rely on what you say, they are more likely to follow along with you.

Create clarity by:

- **Preparing concise, structured messages**
  - o There are three main parts of a good presentation:
    - An opening sequence designed to connect with the audience and establish a clear purpose
    - A middle section that teaches content, normally divided into three or four digestible sections (typically the number of items people can remember easily, and fewer sections help keep the message simple)
    - A clear ending with a focused call to action that asks the audience to take one specific next step rather than several

- **Using simple and direct language**
  - o Avoid jargon and overly flowery language. You don't need to prove how smart you are—succinct phrases will get your message across in the most clear and effective manner. If you can say something in ten words, don't use twenty.
  - o Remember that your audience is most likely not an expert in your field or in the topic; they're here to learn from you. Make sure you're communicating in the language of the audience and not your colleagues.

- **Regularly checking in with your listeners**

  o Just as you seek feedback and confirm satisfaction, make sure your listeners understand what you're saying. Look for subtle nods and engaged audience members.

  o Periodically ask the listener if they have any questions or concerns and address anything that might come up.

- **Reinforcing your key messages multiple times**

  o Note your most important points multiple times throughout your presentation, taking care to connect the main theme with your closing remarks. Don't just say them once and move on, never to remind the listener about them again. If you never revisit them, then maybe they don't support the main theme like you think they do.

- **Creating contrasts**

  o Show both sides of the topic—the "right" way and the "wrong" way, the "before" and the "after"—to illustrate the benefits of the proposed solution and help the listener understand why they need what you're offering.

- **Making good use of the stage and visual aids**

  o Movement from one side of the stage to the other as a presentation progresses creates a visual subconscious cue of improvement or achieving a solution. For example, beginning on the left side of the stage establishes that space as the "before" part of your presentation when people are experiencing their problem. But as you speak, subtly walk to the right side of the stage to create the "after," the golden solution moment when all the audience's problems are solved.

o Align your visuals with your message for consistency and make certain they are not packed with text—if you need one hundred slides filled with words to make your point, your message will get lost, and it'll be clear that you're not clear on what you're trying to say.

o Include visuals beyond just slides—props or handouts—to create engagement and break up potential monotony.

- **Leading with the key points**

o Don't save the best for last. Give the most important information first and name it so. That way, you eliminate any pretense of "hiding" or artificially creating drama for a big reveal.

Trust Cue #5: Voice

If the eyes are the window to the soul, the voice is the comfy chair inviting you to sit and stay a while—or you hope it is.

The way you say things often carries more weight than what you say. If you invite the audience in with your vocal prowess, they're more likely to trust you and follow your advice.

- **Become aware of how you sound**

  o Like a football coach reviewing game tape, if you haven't already, record one of your presentations or speeches and *review the tape*. For the first review, close your eyes and listen to how you sound. For the second review, open your eyes and watch the audience, see how they react to you and your words. Take note when they lean in and really listen and when they're not engaged. These are powerful indicators of when you're at your best or not.

- **Modulate your tone (pitch)**

  o As you're reviewing the tape, pay attention to how your voice naturally (or not) rises and falls, and record yourself practicing those passages, experimenting with adding emotion and emphasis by raising or lowering your voice. See what makes your point more effectively.

  o Additionally, try out a couple vocal warm-ups like humming or lip trilling to loosen up your mouth and voice.

- **Control your pace (speed)**

   o To be an effective speaker, adjust your vocal pacing to the content you're sharing. Practice reading a passage at an intentionally slow pace to become more comfortable with being deliberate and allowing your words to breathe. When you want to get the audience excited, try speaking a little faster. If you want to bring attention to something or pay respect to a particular story, speak a little more slowly.

- **Vary your volume**

   o Like your tone and your pace, regulate your volume. Most people have a natural baseline volume for everyday conversations, but when speaking to a large group, you need to make sure you project (if you have a microphone, you may still need a little extra volume) so the people in the back can clearly hear you. Practice speaking louder when you want to bring attention to something, while speaking more quietly to treat your subject more gently.

- **Take time to pause**

   o Most people are uncomfortable with silence, but adding pauses allows your audience time to catch up with you and your words. Try adding a pause after points you want to emphasize or after emotionally stirring moments. As you practice, exaggerate your pauses to get comfortable with not speaking and still holding audience attention.

Trust Cue #6: Empathy

Empathy is the basis of your emotional connection with the audience. If they feel heard and safe with you, their trust in you will grow.

- **Begin with active listening**
  - o Pay attention to how much you speak versus how much you listen, a balance that is usually easier to achieve in a one-on-one conversation than in a presentation. In that case, add in moments for audience engagement and questions. Hear what the person is saying and show them you hear them—nod your head, lean in, look them in the eye.

- **Validate and reflect others' emotions back to them**
  - o Briefly restate the essence of what someone tells you, including the emotional state, to confirm you heard them. And don't be afraid to ask if you're understanding correctly. It opens the door to having an honest heart-to-heart. If you've misinterpreted part of what they've said, it gives them the chance to correct you. If you've heard it right the first time, when you repeat that

information back to them, they will be encouraged to continue speaking with you.

- **Ask open-ended questions to understand perspectives**

  o As you continue to explore the conversation, using open-ended questions in combination with active listening demonstrates your curiosity in the other person. It shows them that you are invested in them and what they have to say, which helps establish trust. It also allows them to share more information with you than what you could have gotten from leading the conversation with "yes" or "no" questions, information that begins to build an actual relationship with this person. And who knows where that could lead?

- **Practice patience and avoid interrupting**

  o Sometimes a conversation invigorates us so much that we suddenly want to dominate it and share every thought in our head. But don't. Or at least don't do it all at once when the other person is speaking. If you need to, jot down a little note about what you want to say and then lead the conversation back to that thought after the other person has finished. Getting this thought out of your head and onto a note will also allow you to return to active listening rather than wondering when you can insert this idea into the conversation.

- **Respond thoughtfully and sensitively to concerns**

  o Especially if you are in a line-up of speakers, on a panel, or taking over a client from another broker, find a moment to acknowledge those who came before and what they spoke about or did. It can be a great way to tie into a larger conversation or theme, if the event has one. It demonstrates to the audience that you are engaged—we're not so concerned with what we want to say or we're not so important that we miss the contributions of others.

Trust Cue #7: Commonalities

Commonalities create trust through establishing a record of shared past experiences and/or shared values and characteristics, authenticity and credibility, and even empathy. They also enhance comfort, familiarity, and, yes, trust.

- **Identify common ground and highlight shared experiences early in your interactions**

  o When meeting a client for the first time or writing a speech or presentation, take time to learn about them. Check out their professional profiles and find out where they've worked or what they do, where they went to school, and more. In the case of a company, read up on its values. Early on in the conversation or presentation, find ways to identify those shared experiences, values, or knowledge with your listener(s). That can quickly build trust in an initial interaction.

- **Explicitly note shared values or goals**

  o If there isn't a natural way to slip the commonalities into the conversation, tell a story or use a turn of phrase that illustrates or signals those shared values or goals. It could be as simple as saying, "On our way to church last Sunday, my family and I talked about . . ."

- **Leverage mutual connections or networks**

  o Just as you might use recognizable or important names for testimonials to demonstrate your credibility, highlight common connections to create trust through association. Talk about the person who hired you to present if it's a well-known or loved manager or director. Mention any shared group memberships, major sporting events, or even popular films, television shows, or books. Anything that will help the reader understand and connect with you better will go a long way to creating feelings of trust.

- **Adapt language and references to resonate with specific audiences**

  o Describe the problem you address in the language of your audience—not in the way that you, the expert, might talk about it with a colleague, another expert. By adjusting your language and references to align with those of your listener(s), you tap into empathy through reflecting their understanding. Jargon and unfamiliar or inaccessible language can create barriers to understanding. If the audience feels you're out of touch with them or if they can't understand what you're asking them to do, they won't trust you or what you're saying.

- **Say "us" not "I"**

  o Using language that groups you with your audience or listener automatically puts you on the same side. And being on the same team creates a common, uniting experience, which allows trust to grow.

Putting It All Together

Here is a quick list of key elements to include in any presentation to build trust:

- Begin with an opening story that highlights commonalities with the audience.

- Follow the opening with a clear road map, including a specific time commitment.

- During the content teaching, include credibility-building stories that showcase your problem-solving abilities, and share stories of your weaknesses and mistakes to demonstrate authenticity and transparency.

- Throughout the presentation, remain mindful of the context and express empathy for the audience, using their own language.

- At the end, review what you have taught and remind the audience that you have kept your initial promises.

- When you make your call to action, ensure you have woven in stories that establish your credibility in solving their problem, your track record of fulfilling promises, your clear understanding of their needs, and your empathy for their struggles.

Additional Reading

⌄

Conversational Intelligence – Judith Glaser
Explores how language shapes trust, credibility, and relationships.

Crucial Conversations – Kerry Patterson, Joseph Grenny, Ron McMillan, Al Switzler
Shows how clarity and empathy build trust during high-stakes conversations.

"Empathy in the Workplace" – Catalyst Research Report (free online)
Evidence that empathy drives trust and performance.

"How Past Experiences Shape Trust" – Psychology Today (online article)
Discusses how memory and history influence trust decisions.

Influence: The Psychology of Persuasion – Robert Cialdini
Classic research on credibility and commonality in persuasion.

Radical Candor – Kim Scott
Excellent for clarity and empathy in communication.

The Culture Code – Daniel Coyle
Focuses on commonality, belonging, and trust inside high-performing teams.

"The Importance of Common Ground in Communication" – MindTools
Practical resource on creating commonality with others.

"The Link Between Communication and Trust" – Forbes Coaches Council article
Useful overview of clarity, voice, and credibility.

"The Neuroscience of Trust" – Paul J. Zak, *Harvard Business Review*
Research-backed article on building trust at work.

"The Science of Storytelling and Trust" – Paul Zak, *Greater Good Magazine*
Explains how past experiences and shared stories build trust.

Trust: Human Nature and the Reconstitution of Social Order – Francis Fukuyama
Explores trust as the foundation of social and economic prosperity.

Voice Lessons: On Becoming a (Better) Speaker – Nancy Duarte

Insightful for using voice to communicate clarity, trust, and connection.

"What Makes Leaders Credible?" – Kouzes & Posner, *Harvard Business Review*
Key insights on credibility as a driver of trust.

"Why Trust Matters" – David DeSteno, *Scientific American*
Summarizes psychological research on the foundations of trust.

About the Author

Pat Quinn is a master communicator and highly sought-after consultant who has spent over two decades helping people effectively connect with their audiences. He has advised a wide range of top professionals, including professional speakers, pastors, and business leaders, on improving their communication skills and more effectively delivering their critical messages.

A recognized expert in speaking and communication, Pat has coached the biggest names in business, speaking, and sales to help them gain trust quickly and achieve their desired results. Pat Quinn has also developed innovative software tools designed to refine storytelling and significantly improve the quality and trustworthiness of your voice.

For more than 20 years, the world's most influential communicators have relied on Pat Quinn's expertise to design, perfect, and deliver messages that resonate and build lasting trust.